FREE RIDES

paid
$ 4.80

FREE RIDES

HOW TO GET HIGH
WITHOUT DRUGS

Douglas Rushkoff and Patrick Wells

Delta

A Delta Book
Published by
Dell Publishing
a division of
Bantam Doubleday Dell Publishing Group, Inc.
666 Fifth Avenue
New York, New York 10103

BOOK DESIGN – DIANE STEVENSON/SNAP HAUS GRAPHICS

Library of Congress Cataloging in Publication Data

Rushkoff, Douglas.
    Free rides : how to get high without drugs / by Douglas Rushkoff
and Patrick Wells.
      p. cm.
    Includes bibliographical references.
    ISBN 0-385-30331-9
    1. Altered states of consciousness—Problems, exercises, etc.
  2. Meditation. I. Wells, Patrick, 1943–   . II. Title.
  BF1045.A48R87   1991
  154.4—dc20   90-47363   CIP

Manufactured in the United States of America
Published simultaneously in Canada

September 1991

10 9 8 7 6 5 4 3 2 1
RRH

1
INTRODUCTION

How many of you remember childhood afternoons spent whirling on the roundabout in the playground? You'd hold on to it and run so that the whole contraption was spinning. Then you'd jump on and watch the world fly by. Or did you used to hang upside down from a jungle gym to see what people looked like that way? Or stay on the swings, pumping hard to see how high you could get? Or were you the kind of kid who spent your recess listening and spacing out to the echoes and reverberations in a big metal sewer pipe?

These are all examples of self-induced alterations of

consciousness. Highs. Getting high is one of the most natural of human urges. As Andrew Weil explained in *The Natural Mind,* the need for periods of nonordinary consciousness crosses all cultural boundaries and has been observed in children too young to have been influenced by cultural conditioning. It must be a biological urge. While "highs" have gotten a bad reputation in the "just say no" decade, they need not necessarily be associated with drugs or psychedelics. In fact, nonchemical highs are almost invariably more enjoyable, longer lasting, and of greater benefit to one's quality of life.

The problem with drugs is manifold. First, most drugs are simply poisons. They alter your consciousness by screwing you up. Only one category of drugs, psychedelics (which includes marijuana, LSD, and mushrooms) produces what feels like an expanded state of consciousness, but these are limited and precarious experiences at best. Hallucinogens offer only a transitory look at a blissful state of mind. The user must invariably "come down," and without any of the skills necessary to integrate the ecstatic experience into daily life. Thus there is little positive effect to the repeated use of these chemicals. Psychedelics are like window shopping. You get to experience what it must be like to be enlightened but are left wondering how to get there yourself.

The other main problem with chemically induced

states is that it's hard not to associate the drug with the state of consciousness that follows its ingestion. In fact it is not the drug that makes you high. The chemical only acts as a key to opening a state of consciousness that you already have available to you. The repeated use of drugs to unlock that door perpetuates the fiction that you couldn't get there by yourself. You can.

Getting high on your own is like climbing a mountain instead of taking the chairlift. It's a little more difficult, and usually requires the development of one technique or another, but the results are always more grounded and more permanent. Instead of looking out on the mountain from a chair dangling from a wire that someone else erected, you stand on the face of the mountain on your own two feet. Without drugs you are the master of your own experience.

There are, however, many nondrug-related techniques available that result in a variety of different highs. In using any of these methods, it is important to bear in mind that the technique itself is not the high—it's merely opening up a channel to your innate ability to expand your consciousness. The method has no power in itself.

You already know how to get high. You've simply allowed your mind to convince you that you forgot. At one time you were an open channel, receiving signals from everything around you: lights, voices, textures; even thoughts and emotions bombarded you from everywhere. Devoid of judgment, you simply experienced everything and filtered nothing. This was a state of complete awareness and total aliveness. You had no ability or need to concentrate. All senses were alive at once. Growing up, however, you needed to develop the ability to select what you wanted to pay attention to and what you didn't. The mind you developed and carry with you now functions as a filter, enabling you to select certain stimuli and avoid others. This is what allows you to read this book while ignoring people who may be walking around near you, or traffic noise from outside. If you shifted your awareness from the print on this page to the sounds outside, you could completely alter your state of consciousness without even moving a muscle.

So the mind acts like a gatekeeper of awareness, limiting what receives your attention. Employed as your consciousness's receptionist, the mind decides which calls get through and which don't. Most of us, however, have been letting our receptionists make too many of our decisions for us. Our receptionist decides who is worth talking to, who isn't, what we're conscious of and what we're not. Meanwhile we have become prisoners behind our desks, no longer the boss of our office, but the servant of our employee. To us reality is whatever our receptionist chooses for us. Don't misunderstand: the mind is not an evil gatekeeper. It has our best interests at heart; it just gets a little overprotective. The result is that we live in a limited reality.

Getting high is merely moving past the outer office into full-fledged reality. The mind no longer selects and edits what we perceive. Instead we return to the nonjudgmental awareness we had as babies. We no longer rely on our experience or memories to provide appropriate behavior for given circumstances. Rather we respond to every new event as if it were happening for the first time. We are in the moment. We are alive.

The methods for getting past the receptionist vary, but usually involve putting it to sleep, getting it extremely busy, or zoning it out. Often we experience a high during catastrophes. The mind is so busy dealing with danger or disaster that our consciousness is left temporarily unguarded. The next time you hear someone relating a car accident or other life-or-death event, notice how the storyteller seems to fix on strange details—the expression on the driver's face, the tone of a policeman's voice, or even the color of the sky. Unused to unfiltered reality, the freed consciousness doesn't know where to look.

The exhilaration associated with such events often leads sick minds to seek them out. This is the daredevil mentality that motivates benign thrill seeking as well as many violent crimes. The same urge that gets us on a roller coaster leads a less stable individual to drive down city streets at 110 miles per hour. A large part of the attraction to drugs is that we know there is a level of danger in using them. These activities are not what this book is about. Highs do not have to be scary to be fun.

Safe highs allow us to unlock the doors of perception rather than crash through them. The method used is unimportant, as long as it works and it doesn't hurt anybody. We soon realize that highs are not mere vacations from reality. They are excursions *into* reality. Living high becomes the preferred state of being.

In the last chapter, "Staying High," we will explain how peak experiences can be integrated into the rest of your life, but there are a few points about getting high that are worthy of consideration before you get started. Sometimes, because altered states are so much fun, they can make the rest of life seem dull by comparison. This is a mentality to avoid whenever possible. The technique and the state of mind are not the same thing. Any technique, however sacred, is only a vehicle to a place that is already available to you.

It is also easy to allow a given high to overshadow something much greater: truly expanding your consciousness. Highs are great, but they are only a first step in the journey toward full awareness. Peak experiences are rewards along the way, to let you know you are traveling in the right direction. If you are open to highs, let them happen and let them go; you will continue moving toward greater and greater ecstasy. The moment you hold on to a high, try to re-create it, or spend all your conscious time thinking back on it, you are just as stuck as when you began.

Attachments are the opposite of bliss. They are what the mind uses to keep you working at your desk. Concerns like money, outward success, security, or the opinions of others are what the mind clings to and uses to box you in. Don't attach to your highs in this way, or they won't liberate you anymore. You will go on an endless search for new and better highs without ever really feeling satisfied. Altered states of consciousness can teach us how to live in the moment—not some moment that has already passed, however beautiful it may have been.

With this said, then, we embark. This book is not intended as a "how to" guide, but rather as a survey of the kinds of techniques that are available. Before you engage in any of the activities described here, you should seek out a qualified instructor. Under no circumstances should you do any of the activities or exercises without consulting your doctor first. Have fun, laugh at life, but don't be stupid. Enough said.

2
SEEING IS
BELIEVING:
VISUAL HIGHS

The relationship between eyes and highs is obvious. The way things look is often the way we judge whether or not we are in an altered state of consciousness. Things might look clearer, brighter, more three-dimensional, or kinetic. Sometimes we even see things that aren't there. In any case, things often look different when we're high.

One way of getting high on visuals is to look at something that imitates the optic experience of being high. Even if you have not been high before, the brain reacts to the altered vision by producing an appropriate altered consciousness. Some of the techniques in this chapter are simply things to look at, and brief instructions on the best manner in which to view them. These objects or drawings serve to activate the mind like a mantra. Slowly, as you stare, the object will appear to alter. As your vision alters, your mind follows. Most of these techniques exploit the visual center of the brain by manipulating your processing circuitry.

The limbic neocortex is responsible for processing the light our eyes receive into images. It does this is by manipulating a set of about twelve already existing "grids" into a visual language. One of the grids, for example, looks like a field of tiny diamond shapes. Most of the others have not yet been observed individually. Each of these grids could cover your entire field of vision. Any object one looks at is received as a pattern of light by the eyes, then translated into a combination of geometric grids by the brain. Depending upon what you're looking at, any number of these grids may be activated over any portion of your field of vision.

If you gain direct access to the geometric grids of the limbic neocortex, you enjoy control over a usually passive part of the mind. You are in a position to experience the language of the brain on its preconscious level. Even more fascinating, though, is that you are no longer looking at physical reality. You are observing inner space. Many philosophies consider external reality an illusion. This inner space may be the true underlying reality in which consciousness and spirit exist.

At the end of this chapter, we describe techniques that allow you to see things that aren't "really" there. In this way you can expose the brain to visual stimuli that are unavailable in daily life. Concentration on these hitherto unexperienced stimuli brings the mind into new places and the consciousness into new realities.

Have fun with these techniques and, most importantly, go slowly and gently. Never force your eyes—relax them. Your eyes are important to your functioning. Doing anything that causes them pain is probably damaging them, and you should stop if you feel any discomfort.

MANDALAS

Mandalas are complex circular drawings that people look at while they meditate. They are all based on the idea that everything emanates from a center, and throughout nature there are an infinite number of examples of this principle. The petals of a flower emanate from a center. The eye emanates from its iris. A spider web emanates from a central circle. An atom emanates from a nucleus. A solar system emanates from a sun. The reward of mandala work is a deep, intuitive confirmation that the universe emanates from a single source: the mind of God, or the center of life energy.

Carl Gustav Jung was fascinated by mandalas. He observed their occurrence in nearly every culture in the world, from the Navahos to the Tibetans, from the I Ching to Stonehenge, and saw in their repetitive imagery a confirmation of his theory of the collective unconscious. Thus, he surmised, the symbols of the mandala themselves emanate from the core of human consciousness.

The techniques of working with mandalas vary as widely as the mandalas themselves. The simplest would be to find a mandala that you like—for excellent examples see *Mandala* by José and Miriam Arguëlles.

Relax your eyes and look at the image. Gently focus your attention on the center of the circle, but allow your awareness to include the entire mandala. If your consciousness drifts, gently bring it back to just looking at the mandala. After several minutes you can allow your eyes to move slowly around the image, but be sure to avoid sharp, quick eye movements. After you feel you have taken in the entire image, close your eyes and continue to "see" the mandala. You don't need to see it exactly as it looked. You might remember specific images or a generalized pattern. It is not important. After a few minutes of this try to imagine this image as seen by your third eye—the spot on your forehead just above the bridge of your nose, which is thought to be a kind of window to the consciousness. You may need to open your eyes briefly to remember the mandala. Gently focus on your third eye "seeing" the mandala. Finally allow your third eye to become the source of the mandala. It is not only seeing the image but emanating it. Feel the radiance of the mandala move out through your body, into the space around you.

Constructing mandalas is sometimes even more satisfying than meditating on other people's. You can do this by painting, or simply by placing rocks, crystals, or leaves in a circular pattern that pleases you. Children do this all the time. Then do the above steps on your own mandala.

The most intense experience of the mandala would be through a Native American shaman. These medicine men direct groups to create elaborate sand paintings for healing, purification, and consciousness expansion.

MONITOR HIGHS

There are a number of videos and computer-graphics programs out now that use a variety of methods to alter consciousness. The most effective ones either imitate the known geometric grids of the limbic neocortex or work out complex mathematical equations in visual forms. We tend to stay away from most of the New Age stuff out there, which usually involves photography of nature accompanied by soft music. We'd rather just go outside.

As for the former type, they're easy to use. Just shove a tape into the VCR or floppy disk into the computer and go. We recommend turning off all the lights in the room. Most of these videos have soundtracks, but if you don't like their music, try your own or watch in silence.

Our favorite tapes are computer generated and based on fractal equations. They look great and seem to resonate with something deep in the consciousness. In fact fractals are simple math equations, such as $y = x^2 + 6$. For every input, x, there is an output, y. But instead of just graphing the resulting parabola, for a fractal each y value is plugged back into the equation as a new x. Then that answer is plugged back into the equation and so on. The amazing thing about fractal equations is that they can explain nature. The pattern of growth of a fern, for example, can be entirely explained by about two fractal equations. More advanced ones can explain how cells differentiate in an embryo. In short they are mathematical representations of the process of life.

The equations would normally be graphed on a three-dimensional axis, but since television has a two-dimensional screen, the depth of a given point is defined by its color. This results in wonderful landscapes of color,

which are at once abstract and organic. They must be seen.
The best fractal tapes are available through Fractalvision,
P.O. Box 1193, Agoura Hills, California 91376 (818-889-
5425). Ask for *Fractalidescope* by Arnie Greif, or *Fractal
Fantasy* by Charlie Fitch. Aeon Home Video has a new
video on the market called *Fractal Lumination Volume 1*. It
features a score by Moody Blues, and a portion of the
profits go to a reforestation charity. It's available by calling
800-ROCK ART.

Fractals, which are designed on a computer, can be
viewed far better on a high-resolution computer monitor.
A program called *Fractools* was created to allow you to
generate your own fractals or manipulate images from a
library on disk. Effects available include "strobe," "kalei-
doscope," "stained glass," and "mouse movies." You need
an IBM computer, an EGA or VGA monitor, and a hard
disk. For more information call Bourbaki Inc, 800-289-
1347.

The very best computer graphics programs, however, are made for the MacIntosh. Todd Rundgren, mu-
sician cum computer hacker, has designed a stunningly
beautiful screensaver program called *Flofazer*. Its official
purpose is to protect your computer screen after you've
left your system unattended; its true purpose is to dazzle
you into altered states with swirling, colorful imagery.
These pictures are *nice*. Rundgren has designed about

thirty different patterns to choose from, and while a color monitor is not essential, it is 90 percent of the fun. These are the best visuals available anywhere. *Flofazer* is a masterpiece. Rundgren is a genius. Get the program directly from Todd at Utopia Grokware, 415-331-0714. An IBM version is also in the works.

Other kinds of mind-altering videos are created using optics, video feedback, and manipulation of raw images. They are sometimes billed as "guided meditations," like Shirley MacLaine's *Inner Workout,* but many are available with no talk. Ken Jenkins, the artist who created the effects for MacLaine's video, has several of his own works. The best is probably *Illuminations*. It's a very smooth-flowing study of light and color. Unlike the fractal videos, *Illuminations* is seamless, and allows you to float much longer. Most of the people who watch it have a Rorschack-type reaction and see angels or spaceships or parts of the body. It's available at most New Age bookstores or through Immediate Future Productions, P.O. Box 1341, Los Altos, California 94023 (415-948-7834).

There are many videos to choose from. The following is a brief list of some I can recommend:

The Experiment at Petaluma is Terence McKenna's long-awaited venture into psychedelic videography. It is billed as "an alchemical computer assemblage of thought, sound, and image" and is quite successful at re-creating stimulating visuals. Send $32.95 to ROSE X, Box 728, Petaluma, California 94953.

California Images is a collection of twenty short pieces by California's top video artists. None are really long enough to take you in completely, but the video would be a good starting place if you are trying to find out what kinds of video work best for you. Contact Pilot Video, 425 Alabama Street, San Francisco, California 94110 (415-863-3555).

Structures from Silence is a set of motion paintings by Marianne Dolan. Her description is probably best: "Join a dreamflight through liquid time when starfields shift, clouds implode and quivering plasma galaxies swell and are born." Contact the Ark Group, P.O. Box 410685, San Francisco, California 94141-0685 (800-727-0009).

There are also several feature films on tape that produce vivid altered states of consciousness when viewed with that purpose. Take the phone off the hook, get a comfortable chair, clear your mind, and relax deeply into the imagery on screen. Don't worry about plot and character. Just watch the images, the faces of characters, the movement of the camera, and the changes of scenery.

We have found documentaries often work the best. You are watching real people behave, without having to be there. The perspective is novel. Try documentaries that aren't in English. Even animal or nature documentaries work as long as the filmmakers haven't imposed a story or strong sensibility of their own onto the images. Usually simple, repetitive tasks on film work the best—like a documentary on Indians building canoes or the workings of a mannequin factory. Werner Herzog produced some excellent documentaries early in his career, but most are not available on videotape. Godfrey Reggio's *Koyaanisqatsi* and *Powaqqatsi* are both available on tape and combine time-elapsed imagery, live-action footage, and Philip Glass music.

Animated features like *Fantastic Planet* and *Light Years* have a science fiction emphasis but also provide some stunningly simple visuals. Check your local video store for these or other weird films and view them with the intention of melding with the imagery. Simply relax your consciousness to conform with the film and get high without chemicals.

Also watch your local revival house's listings for a film called *The Valley,* about a group of Europeans who go to an Indonesian island looking for exotic feathers. They find, instead, a very strange tribe and end up getting involved in their rituals. Apparently the group of actors making the film had a parallel experience as they shot the footage. The result is spectacularly mind-altering. The score is by Pink Floyd.

Sometimes the manner in which films are projected can affect you greatly. If you haven't been to an Imax theater, check that out. The screen is huge, and because of the way the seats are situated, you feel the illusion of motion. Go when they are showing a film about flying and see how "into it" you can get. Try going with a group of similarly minded friends, so you don't feel as strange falling into your own world as you watch.

Most planetariums now do laser shows on weekend evenings. Don't talk to anyone. Just breathe, relax, and look up.

STROBES

Pick up a strobe light at Radio Shack, a gift shop, a theater-lighting store, or your neighborhood head shop. It should cost under thirty dollars. A strobe is a xenon tube, which charges and decharges very quickly and completely. Unlike an incandescent bulb, which fades out when you turn it off, a xenon bulb does not ghost. It goes out immediately. This makes it ideal for creating a strobe effect.

If you can't find or afford a strobe light, find the most directed and clear light you can. Some kind of spotlight would be ideal. It should be a lamp from which no light would escape if you were to cover the opening with your hand. Put a large fan directly in front of the light, so that the flow of light is interrupted every time a blade of the fan swings by.

Go to a pitch-black room (use a closet if you must) where you can sit down comfortably three to eight feet away from your strobe light, which should be placed at eye level. Turn it on so that it flashes at a rate of somewhere between ten and twenty flashes a second. If you're using a fan, put it on a slow speed. Stare directly at the bulb, leaving your eyes gently out of focus. If your eyes are sensitive, try putting a blue gel in front of the bulb. As you sit and stare, you may notice a strange luminescent shape form between you and the light. We usually see it as a purplish glow, but it may look different to you. Concentrate on the apparition if one appears. Relax and wait.

PHOSPHENE STIMULATION

This is something most of us did as kids before we fell asleep at night, but has now become a lost art to us. It is an easy and effective way to reach extraordinarily altered states of consciousness and is practiced by shamans and monks alike. Some sects regard it as such a powerful technique that they disclose it only to trusted students. If you can be trusted, continue reading.

Wash your hands and face well. Sit with your eyes closed and gently press your closed lids with your fingers. Observe the colored or black spots that appear. Concentrate on these shapes as a meditation, or continue to manipulate with your fingers and watch them change.

LIFE IN SOFT FOCUS

The next time you are outside in a nonthreatening environment (where there aren't cars to run you over or cliffs to fall off), try this technique. There are shamans who say this is the only technique needed to reach complete enlightenment.

Sitting or standing, very softly focus on a point ahead of you. Let your eyes relax so that the point you are looking at gets fuzzy. Without moving your eyes, shift your attention to your peripheral vision. Let your eyes gently rest on the point ahead of you while you place all of your awareness toward your sides. If it helps, put your arms in front of you and slowly spread them out to the edge of your field of vision. Wave your hands if you need to, but don't move your eyes to find them. Resist for as long as possible the temptation to focus your eyes.

SEEING WHAT ISN'T THERE

We've saved this for last because this is the good stuff. We've been practicing these techniques for years now on our own, but found a good little book in our research that outlines much of what we discovered. It's called *Little Manual for Players of the Glass Bead Game,* by George Pennington.

We often use a technique that goes something like this: Put two pennies on a table, equally lit, in the same position about two inches apart. Look down at them and unfocus your eyes by slightly crossing them. Do this by relaxing the eye muscles, not tensing them. The pennies will turn into double images as they move out of focus. By gently manipulating your eye focus, connect the shifting image of the left penny with the one on the right so that it appears as if you are looking at three pennies. Keep working at it until you have aligned them perfectly. Then just stare at the middle image. It will seem brighter, more radiant than either of the "real ones." In fact the side pennies might appear to become white or transparent.

Pennington has a very similar exercise in his book, in which you use your thumbs instead of pennies. We tried this, and we like it even more. You hold your thumbs out in front of you, about two inches apart, and unfocus (cross) your eyes to create at first two "inner" thumbs, then overlap them to make a single third thumb. This thumb will appear more lifelike than either of your "real" ones. It will seem to emanate a life force.

After you've gotten good enough to be able to maintain this for a minute or so, play with it. Manipulate the thumbs in different ways and see what happens. Try the same thing with penny-size dots drawn on a piece of paper. Use two different colors and combine them in a central dot. This two-colored dot (you'll have to see it to know what we mean) seems to float above the page on which the real dots are drawn. The possibilities are endless.

The magic of this technique is that the illusion appears more "real" than reality. This casts an interesting light on the dimension in which we live. Our physical reality and all that we see may be just a projection from somewhere else—some source of everything. We play out life on a "holodeck"★ of sorts. By creating our own illusion, that of a third thumb for example, we come into direct contact with that interface.

Do pick up a copy of Pennington's book if you'd like to try more exercises or his visual version of the "Glass Bead Game." Or go back to Carlos Castaneda's *Journey to Ixtlan* to try some of Don Juan's techniques. The most all-encompassing source of visual hallucinatory techniques can be found in Pierre Derlon's *Secrets Oubliés des Derniers Initiés Gitans*.

★*Star Trek: The Next Generation* provides its characters with a unique form of recreation: a "holodeck." This is a large room where elaborate, moving, physical holograms are projected in three dimensions so that people can interact with them. A person might choose, for example, to play Sherlock Holmes. The computer will then create nineteenth-century England and the characters necessary to play out the mystery.

3
SOUNDS
GOOD TO ME

The most common way people get high today is through music. We are so inundated with music that we hardly realize the profound effect it has on our states of mind. Music has been shown to have a marked impact on the ill, the emotionally disturbed, the mentally disabled, and even the profoundly insane. Music can increase the growth of plants or even the activity of yogurt cultures. As we all know by now, music—and sound itself—is a powerful tool for altering consciousness.

Sound has been abused by those who understand it. Muzak has been proven to make us buy things. White noise can increase productivity in the workplace. Annoying sounds are made to emanate from certain areas of shopping malls to help corral people into the stores.

With a fraction of the knowledge needed to exploit sound in these ways, each of us can develop an extremely powerful tool for controlling our own states of mind and level of consciousness. By making music, creating sound, or listening to the sounds and music of others, we can get very, very high.

HOW SOUND WORKS

Sound is a wave form. Mathematically, in three dimensions, a sound wave looks like a stretched-out Slinky toy. The frequency of the sound is represented by how many loops the spiral makes in a given length of wire. Sound waves affect us in a real, organic way. They are not just ideas. They are physical events. Sound waves enter through the ears (as well as through the rest of the body as vibration) and move parts of our brain. Sound has a direct effect on the way our brain functions. It is a physical tool, in the shape of a spiral, that can enter through our ears and create waves in our brain.

Different sound waves have different qualities. A bell will create a very smooth, round wave—the open sound is thus soothing to the brain. An alarm-clock buzz creates what we call a sawtooth wave, which looks like the sharp teeth of a saw. Its effect on the brain, then, is correspondingly uncomfortable.

Any shape of sound wave can also have any frequency. Certain frequencies will sound good together, and others will not. Sympathetic frequencies, the kind that sound good, usually share some of the spirals of the Slinky. There is overlap every few turns. In other words, each four turns of one spiral will correspond with exactly eight turns of another. The brain can recognize the patterning and align itself fairly easily. If two frequencies seem unrelated to the brain, it will not know how to "fix" or resolve the frequencies.

The same is true for the overall rhythm of sounds. We can hear rhythm in repeating patterns. This is the way musicians are able to write their music down on paper. They start by setting up rules such as "every measure will have four beats." This creates a song with a repeating pattern of four beats. The brain has something to hook on to.

When the brain feels comfortable with a sound, it allows the sound deep inside. This is the important part. Once a sound gets inside a person, the person naturally resonates with that sound. This is an organic resonance—it is more than just a "feeling." The organic resonance touches the very core of one's being.

There are various ways to resonate. You can do so either by producing sound or by just listening. The effects are different, but all quite interesting. Sound was our first experience of greater consciousness. It is one of the tools we still regularly use to open ourselves to new kinds of awareness.

MAKING SOUND

With nothing more than a pot and a spoon you can reach places you thought were reserved for monks. With a few other props, you can sing with the angels. But the first and primary musical instrument is the human voice. Your voice is all you need to reach bliss.

The easiest way to start using your voice is by chanting sounds such as mantras. We know, you do not like meditation. Fine. Don't think of this as meditation. The first obstacle to get over is fear of making sound. Start by making sounds where you cannot be heard. (This is why so many people sing in the shower. They think that the noise of the water is drowning out their voices.) Go to a good, resonant place. If there is no empty cathedral or warehouse readily accessible, find a garage, a tunnel, or even a porcelain bathroom. Sit and listen for a while. Relax.

Lie on your back. Begin by watching your breath. Breathe with your mouth open. Then, very slowly, allow your breath to activate your vocal chords. On each exhale relax into a *huh* sound. You can slowly let this turn into a *huh-yuh-yuh-yuh* sound. Just feel the way the sound moves through your body. Make this as effortless as possible. Do this for as long as you can stand it. Your mind might start to move just from this.

Try standing. Tilt your head back, opening your jaw all the way. Allow a wide-open *hah* sound to come out. Hold the sound for as long as you can (but don't force anything). Once you feel comfortable with these simple sounds, allow yourself to do a simple chant. Stand up straight, look forward, and make the sound *OM*. Broken up into parts, the *OM* sound is actually *AH-OH-UUMMMM*. Make this sound at various pitches.

Once you have experienced anything at all, take yourself through the next stages. Experiment. Try sitting, standing, or moving. Use different pitches, sounds, and tempos. Open and close your eyes. The possibilities are endless.

CHORDS

Next bring your friends. Many people have experienced their first highs making group chords. Unlike the rigid rules of a junior high school chorus, the techniques of chording are very freestyle. Stand with a group of people—the more the better—in a big circle. You can do this anywhere. Each in your own time make the *AHH* sound. Do not worry about singing in any standard harmony. Just sing out. Let the chord go on for as long as it wants to. Amazingly enough, most of the time everyone will stop at once anyway, with no prodding. A chord can last ten minutes or an hour.

As with any sound making, the most important thing is to listen. Your consciousness will not change if it is not open. In this case you must be open to the sound. This means that you need to relax and listen. Do not bear down on your own sound. Listen and resonate with the sound that is around you.

SOUND WITH PROPS

The best course we took at Princeton was labeled "Clap for Credit" by its detractors. It was taught by a genius who showed his students how to listen. He set up a table with kitchen utensils, made each student take one, turned off the lights, and told everyone to listen and make sound. It was as easy—or as difficult—as that. The results were amazing.

We have all been at parties that devolved into improvisational jazz sessions in the kitchen. Try the same thing, except begin gently. Listen to every sound. Create a fabric of resonances that intertwine with each other. You can graduate to tribal instruments such as drums, kalimbas, flutes, and bells if you wish. But remember, you are not playing instruments in order to make music. You are just playing and listening.

The quality of this play should be like when a baby learns to make a new sound. It will repeat this sound for what seems like hours on end. The baby is simply fascinated by the way the sound *feels*. The baby is getting off on sound.

This sounds too easy, we know, but look at every collection of monks, any tribe, or any group of babies. Sound is the way they alter consciousness. They chant, sing, or bang on things to get high.

The highest our friend, Jamie, ever got chanting was when he joined a group who performed the Balinese Monkey Chant (the Ketjak). Admittedly not everyone has an Indonesian chorus in his or her backyard, but many universities now have international music as part of their curriculum. See what is available. African and West Indian music is equally expanding. Most teachers of ethnic music will let you join their classes whether or not you are a student of the university. You can certainly take part in extracurricular performances.

TUNING FORKS

One slightly more organized but equally effective sound technique uses tuning forks to create resonance. You need to purchase a set of forks, one for each note of the scale. Buy aluminum ones because they are cheaper and a little easier to use. Lay them out in front of you in order, from lowest to highest. Sit in front of them. The way to operate a tuning fork is to take it by the handle with two or three fingers and tap the other end against your knee. Do not hit it against a table or hard surface, because the fork will ring a second, slightly annoying, tone.

Try the lowest fork first. Hit it against your knee and bring it about two inches from your ear. If you are not sure that you are hearing the tone, hit the fork against your knee again and set the handle against your forehead. Hear that? The way to alter consciousness with tuning forks is to combine frequencies. Certain intervals work better than others. Try the lowest and the highest first. They should be exactly an octave apart. Hold one in the left and one in the right hand, hit them against your knees, and bring

★

.

★

them up to your ears. Try moving them around your head. Then try different combinations.

OTHER INSTRUMENTS

The number of easy, consciousness-altering instruments out there is almost endless. Try bells, gongs, xylophones, chimes, drums, or anything that looks fairly resonant and easy to play. There are a few good books on making music. Most of them are written for nursery school teachers and can be found in the appropriate section in the library. You might also try *Music and Sound in the Healing Arts* by John Beaulieu.

SYNCHRONICITY

These tapes, also called the Brother Charles tapes, are not music, so they need a category of their own. They are part of a program designed to help people evolve their consciousness. The tapes available to the public are pretty powerful indicators that Brother Charles is on to something.

The tapes work by synchronizing the left and right hemispheres of the brain through sound. You must wear stereo headphones to listen to the cassettes. There are different cassettes to bring you to different brain states. The most basic ones are $25 each, and available through MSH Association, Route 1, Box 192-B, Faber, Virginia 22938 (800-962-2033). We have tried only one, called *Om Mani Padme Hum*, based on the Buddhist chant. It definitely works for us, bringing us to a deep meditative state within a minute or two. These tapes are more than just music. They "meditate" you, even if you do not know how. They were created to bring meditation to Westerners who do not seem capable of developing the patience to meditate the old-fashioned way.

To really get the benefit from these tapes, you should probably join the whole MSH program. You take a course through the mail. They save the advanced stuff for their official students. The people we know who have subscribed to the course swear by it. They say it gets them higher than anything they have done before, with greater understanding of the process of full awakening. The main course, *Recognitions*, costs about $350 and takes three months. They send you a bunch of tapes and materials and talk to you on the phone. If you have the inclination, try it out. This is not a rip-off.

BUYING MUSIC

Now that high fidelity is readily accessible on a decent Walkman, most anyone can purchase a decent high on cassette. The rest of this chapter amounts to a list of music that gets you high. We tend to stick to the more esoteric tribal music. Anything Indonesian, African, Indian, West Indian, or ancient usually works for us. Many people also get great results from electronic and New Age music. You can get high from any kind of music. We are sure there are people who get high off Duran Duran. If you have a favorite kind of music, that's fine. But you may be too familiar with that kind of sound for it to be an effective consciousness changer. If you have been getting off on Mozart for the last twenty years, chances are the patterns it creates in your brain are almost standard by now—euphoric perhaps, but standard.

The way to use music to change consciousness is to bring new resonances to the brain. New rhythms and textures create new patterns. Thrown off balance, even temporarily, the mind gets busy. It frees the consciousness to explore new territory. Live music, of course, is always better than recorded, but on nights when there is just nowhere to go and nothing to do, turn to your stereo.

Go to the biggest or weirdest record store in your

neighborhood and browse along the shelves. Check the international section and the New Age records. The best twenty-five that we know of for altering consciousness are the following:

1 Any good Buddhist "overtone" chanting. These guys sing more than one note at a time. The best we know of are the Gyuto monks on Windham Hill Records.

2 The Balinese Monkey Chant. This gets pretty ferocious. In Bali, art and everyday life are one thing. The performers are just people, but boy can they make a lot of sound.

3 The Grateful Dead. Find a Deadhead and ask him to play you his favorite concert tape. Tell him you want to listen to *Darkstar* or *Morning Dew*. Make sure it's from a concert near 1970–72, when they were still touring with the "wall of sound" amplification system. If you don't know the Dead, have an open mind. There's a reason they are still the number-one touring band in the country after twenty years. (Our friend Bernie says that "China Cat Sunflower" from the 1972 European tour album gives an excellent head rush.)

4 Any good dervish music. Try the *Dhikr of the Halveti-jerrahi Dervishes*.

5 African drums. Play this loud and through speakers. Find *Drums of Passion*, which is African tam-tams, or any nonanthropological African-drum record. The problem with the scientific ones is that they play only thirty seconds of each rhythm.

6 Bulgarian music. This is a new rage (they used some in a TV commercial, so it must be mind-altering). The Bulgarian State Radio and Television Female Vocal Choir has recorded two albums, *Le Mystère des Voix Bulgares*, volumes 1 and 2.

7 Brian Eno. We know. Eno. Not only does his name spell "one" backward but his "Ambient" records (particularly numbers 2 and 3) are stunning examples of how music, even when it's *intended* to do so, can alter your consciousness.

8 Tony Scott. You don't have to be meditating to audition his *Music for Zen Meditation* or *Music for Yogic Meditation*. Don't condemn this because it sounds like New Age stuff.

9 John McLaughlin and Pat Metheny. We put them into one category because they are both guitarists. Check out McLaughlin's *Shakti*, and Metheny's *As Falls Wichita* . . . albums. They are not the kinds of albums you would expect from guitarists.

10 *Yamantaka* is a collaborative effort of modern and traditional artists working with chimes, bells, and gamelan to create the weirdest, most ethereal sounds they can. This one works.

11 Music of Native Americans. Some people tell us these records bring out terrible feelings of guilt and remorse. Still, though there are not many natives left in America, there are numerous albums worth your while. Again, be sure the cuts are longer than a minute or two.

12 Real World Music is a new branch of Virgin Records dedicated to recording traditional and modern music from around the world. Peter Gabriel is one of the producers of this series of fine recordings from Asia, Africa, and Europe.

13 Iascos and Constance Demby wrote the music for the video *Illumination* and have albums of their own that are equally evocative. This is New Age–type music.

14 "Marcey" is a woman who, after facing a life-threatening accident, began to create electronic music that has done everything from healing to bringing people out-of-body. Her tapes are available through her own company. Contact: P.O. Box 830495, Richardson, Texas 75080 (214-690-3556). These composi-

tions evoke a very different experience from most New Age music and bring the listener very close to the trance state Marcey was in when she wrote them.

15 *Music of the Pygmies* (Ocora) is a record of mostly chanting. The cover is neat, and the Pygmies have very unusual voices, tones, and rhythms.

16 Indian Music. Find any traditional ragas, kirtans, and bhajans, such as those on *Introduction to Indian Classical Music* or *Classical Ragas of India*.

17 Anything by Vangelis. People who like synthesizer music probably already know most of his work. His earlier recordings are more trippy than his later albums and film scores (avoid things like *Chariots of Fire*).

18 *The Kodo Heartbeat Drummers of Japan* is pretty fabulous on CD—the dynamic range is just a little too wide for cassette. These guys chant and bang loudly. The cumulative effect is thrilling. Get the tape only if you cannot stand CDs.

19 *Holophonics Live!* is an album that was put out by the *Brain-Mind Bulletin*. It is a full dose of a wide variety of mind-altering sounds. Holophonics is based on the work of Hugo Zucarelli, who understood sound as a holographic experience of the mind. His sound–effects

experiments challenge what we thought were the limits of recorded sound.

20 Ray Lynch's album *The Sky of the Mind* has some excellent Tibetan-bell music. The recording is great for opening up to sustained tones and resonances. Almost any Tibetan-bell music will be quite effective in bringing about changes in your mental state.

21 Steve Reich's music is often compared to Philip Glass's, but is much better for our purposes. He takes a line of music and slowly alters it as it repeats. The effect is not spacey—it is involving and awakening. You have to be conscious to listen to this music. Try *Tehillin*, which is mostly voices.

22 Richard Burmer sounds pretty middle-of-the-road New Age to us, but he does seem to be a favorite among the people we know who use music to alter consciousness. His *Bhakti Point* is intended to be "a musical journey to an imaginary paradise."

23 Gamelan. This is music from Indonesia played on instruments that look like short, squat xylophones. The gamelan scale is different from the eight-note chromatic scale we are used to and tends to retrain the mind into new patterns of awareness.

24 Haitian voodoo music. If you can get over the false notion that voodoo means black magic, you will find a treasure of mind-altering sounds here. Haitian drum music is very different from the African tam-tam mentioned above.

25 Wildlife. There are several good recordings of the music of whales and dolphins that can bring out a tremendous feeling of compassion and warmth. Also try recordings of the sounds of jungles, rain forests, and deep woods. Of course these recordings are only the next best thing to being there.

4
TAKE A DEEP
BREATH

The breath is a fascinating thing. It is one of the only processes in the body that can be either consciously or unconsciously controlled. That is, if you do not think about it, you will breathe naturally. You breathe this way in your sleep. Your breathing is as unconscious as your heartbeat or the function of your spleen. But you also have the ability to control your breath purposefully. You can hold your breath, breathe more or less deeply, more or less rapidly, through your nose or your mouth, in one way and out the other, in special rhythms—the list is nearly endless.

Because the breath can be either conscious or unconscious, it becomes a gateway for these two parts of yourself. Your breath is the link between your waking state and the myriad other states of consciousness. By breathing consciously, you bring into current experience that which is usually reserved for the subconscious. Thus you gain easy access to a number of highs.

These techniques have been practiced for centuries in pranayama, the yoga of breathing. Current work in the field, led by Stanislav Grof, uses breathing for psychiatric therapy and "rebirthing."

PRANAYAMA

Pranayama is taken from two Indian words. The first, *prana*, stand for roughly the Indian equivalent of the Taoist *chi*. It means "life energy, or cosmic energy." It is the stuff that makes everything go. *Ayama* means conscious control. Pranayama is the conscious control of the cosmic energies. One major access to the prana is through the air, so pranayama uses breathing techniques to develop a larger store of prana in the practitioner.

Prana is conducted through negative ions in the air. (Later we will consider ionizers and their effect on consciousness.) This is important to know, because the pranayama exercises will work better in an area more densely populated with these healthy ions. The easiest way to judge if air is properly charged is how you feel when you inhale it. You are not likely to find many negative ions in an office building or on a polluted freeway. On the other hand, if you do breathing exercises on a beach or in the plains, you will have far better results. Find the best place you can.

An excellent book on pranayama is B.K.S. Iyengar's *Light on Pranayama.* The best source of pranayama practices is André van Lysebeth's *Pranayama: The Yoga of Breathing.* Following are a few of the basic kinds of methods you can find in his book or at a beginning class, ending in an advanced exercise that should bring you quickly into an altered state of consciousness. Again, we encourage you to find a qualified instructor before trying these exercises. Read these descriptions to determine whether or not pranayama is the kind of technique you wish to pursue.

A PRANAYAMA EXERCISE

The point of focus in these exercises is the olfactory region at the roof of the first sinus cavity, just inside your skull. This is the place where air can go directly to your brain. To get a sense of this area, smell or imagine smelling something sweet like a flower. The place where you perceive the sweetness of the scent is the olfactory region.

Try breathing through your nose, allowing as much air to contact this region as possible. It will be helpful to "hold" (not with your hands but with the muscles in your nose) your nostrils open while doing so.

After you are confident that you are experiencing your breath in this way, try adding a visualization. Imagine that energy rises up along the back of your spine with every inhalation. It may eventually manifest as a warm, tingly feeling traveling up your back to your skull. You may want to visualize this as a color, light, force—it does not matter.

Be sure to think of your abdomen as the motivator of your breath. Most of us breathe from our chests. This is shallow breathing. As you breathe in, your abdomen should expand. Do not force it to distend. If you imagine that air enters you like milk being poured into a bottle, you will see how air fills you from the bottom up. Eventually you should begin to feel your bottom back ribs expanding as you inhale and coming together slightly as you exhale. If your breathing is tense and this sensation is unavailable to you, consult Kristin Linklater's *Freeing the Natural Voice* (New York: Drama Book Publishers, 1976). The first chapters are a lesson plan designed to help you breathe this way. The Linklater technique is the best method known for freeing up a channel for air.

So now you are breathing consciously, through your

open nose, stimulating the olfactory center, and visualizing energy traveling up your spine. The last of the basic techniques to add on is called alternate-nostril breathing. Quite simply it means breathing in and out through one nostril, then in and out through the other. You close your right nostril with the thumb of your right hand, breathe in through your left nostril, then breathe out again through the left. Now open your right nostril, and close the left one using your index and/or middle finger. Then inhale through the right nostril and exhale through the left. The idea is to practice alternate-nostril breathing, along with the other techniques, until you can do them without thinking.

RHYTHMIC BREATHING

The first specific exercise a pranayama student learns is rhythmic breathing. You must not work too hard to get it right, which would only cause you to be more tense. An instructor would have you begin by exhaling through both nostrils. Then you would inhale through the left nostril, holding the right with the thumb of your right hand, as in alternate-nostril breathing, above, counting "one one thousand, two one thousand" and exhale again through the left counting "one one thousand, two one thousand, three one thousand, four one thousand." In other words, you breathe in a relaxed fashion but with the exhalations taking twice as long as the inhalations. You would practice alternating nostrils according to this rhythm, in and out through one nostril, then in and out through the other.

As you got better at this, you would try increasing the length of each inhalation and exhalation, as long as they stay in the same ratio of one beat inhaling to every two beats exhaling. This exercise, properly done, is extremely powerful. Most teachers request that you do it sitting up straight, preferably on the floor.

BETWEEN THE INHALATION AND EXHALATION

Once you have mastered the above technique, your instructor could teach you the more advanced practice of holding your breath. You start by doing everything outlined above. You are now breathing rhythmically and alternately, two beats in and four beats out. Now when you inhale, retain the breath in your lungs for eight counts—that is, twice the length of an exhalation. If you feel yourself getting tense, you shorten the rest of your cycle. If you need to, just count one beat on the inhalation, four with the breath held, and two on the exhalation. You slowly increase the amount of time you can effortlessly hold in your breath.

This place, between the inhalation and the exhalation, is where we have experienced the most profound alterations of consciousness. After a while it is as if you forget to breathe. You feel your blood circulating around your body in a different way.

Breath retention itself is an extremely advanced pranayama technique. After getting proper instruction, you can practice this on your own, as long as you stay gentle and effortless with yourself. The trick is not to take one deep breath and hold it but to breathe deeply for a while and just hold the last in the series of inhalations. To learn about more advanced techniques, call the yoga schools in your area to see which offer pranayama classes, or consult Lysebeth's book.

HOLOTROPIC BREATHING

In the 1960s, psychedelics were used in psychiatric therapy to alter consciousness and help people redefine the arbitrary and sometimes limiting structures around their experience of life. A session would last several hours and take the form of a "trip" with professional guidance.

When these chemicals became illegal, doctors developed other techniques to provide an intense experience of psycho-spiritual catharsis and resolution. Stanislav Grof and his wife, Christina, came up with something called holotropic breathing. They and other therapists have been using this technique for years now, with very impressive results. Techniques very similar to theirs are also employed in a system called Rebirthing, which, as the name implies, involves reliving the birth trauma.

The Grofs do their technique in groups. They set up a large, safe room, play some evocative music, and tell their patients to lie on their backs and breathe deeply for half an hour or so. As simple as it sounds, this is the entire technique, and it works! The patients go through the full range of transpersonal experiences, ranging from time and space alteration to visits with spirit guides. Some begin to sing and chant, some go into past-life regressions, and others just get very high.

The Grofs hypothesize that holotropic breathing awakens some of the anxieties experienced by the fetus in the birth canal. The character of your birth experience has, according to the Grofs, colored perceptions throughout the rest of your life. Holotropic-breathing therapy has been designed to help people explore the way their worldview has been limited and how these limitations have in turn created unwanted patterns in their thinking and behavior.

Rebirthers use very similar techniques, but in a one-on-one session. They do more hands-on work with their clients, helping them through the rebirthing process. The client lies on something like a massage table, and the whole setup is much more like a healing session. Our problem with the rebirthing people is that their work is often tied to a huge set of doctrines about human experience. Rebirthers seem to be promoting their own way of looking at the world. To us this seems an unnecessary adjunct to the technique. Still, there are many qualified rebirthers practicing throughout the United States. Most New Age periodicals carry advertisements for rebirthers.

Holotropic-breathing therapists, on the other hand, have no particular agenda. To learn more about the technique, see the Grofs' book *The Adventure of Self-Discovery*.

In any event, only do holotropic breathing or birthing under the supervision of a licensed psychotherapist or practitioner. Although the technique is easy to do at home, the repercussions are not so easy to handle. We cannot overemphasize the power of these techniques. They serve as absolute proof that profoundly intense psychedelic experiences are available without chemicals.

HIGH ALTITUDE

Many people get high when they go to high places. Once you get up about 10,000 feet above sea level, you may experience remarkable alterations in your consciousness. Rather than driving up a mountain road, it is preferable to go up all at once, either in a helicopter or on a skylift. Most mountain ranges have facilities like this for tourists.

The vast majority of people who go to these places experience highs that they ignore. They assume they are sick or merely inspired by the beautiful view. Those of us who understand consciousness, however, recognize the light-headedness and accompanying clarity as something else. When you are sick, you experience a change in physical sensations, but you lose clarity of thinking. When you are high, you experience a physical change, too, but thoughts seem to be clearer. Being open to what high altitude can do to you is half the technique.

So go with what you are feeling. It may seem subtle at first, but it will get very extreme very soon. We have seen people weeping, laughing, and dancing from high-altitude consciousness work. If you start feeling too high or that you are going to faint, just sit down and breathe slowly. It should pass (seek help if it doesn't). Most of getting high has to do with being open to the experience.

Do not complicate your high-altitude experience with the ingestion of any chemicals, even alcohol. This is extraordinarily dangerous, especially because in thin air chemicals will affect your body differently. The most intense chemicals we would ever take during a high-altitude rush are tea and doughnuts.

After you are in your high-altitude altered state, observe your perceptive abilities. Look around you. Your vision and hearing will be sharp. Try talking or singing.

Notice how different you sound to yourself, especially in comparison with the way other people and things sound. Feel free to do one of the meditations described in later chapters. Do anything you like, as long as it is not strenuous.

The high-altitude high comes on subtly, but it is very, very penetrating. Do not break its force by engaging in extreme activities of any sort. Just walk or sit, look around, and breathe.

NEGATIVE IONS

Negative ions are in the air. They are healthy and cleansing and are thought to transmit the energy of life and light. They occur naturally in the air and are found in higher concentration near the ocean or in open plains than they are in the mountains and lush woods. They are hardly found at all in cities, office buildings, or homes made of modern materials.

Metal neutralizes the charge of negative ions. Air that passes through a heating duct contacts the metal. By the time it gets from a furnace or air conditioner to you, it has no negative ions left. The places in which we spend most of our time act like faraday cages, blocking out the negatively charged particles that can give us vitality, clarity, and emotional sanity.

To replace the depleted negative ions—at least indoors—several machines called ionizers are available for anywhere between $40 and $100 or more. These are not air purifiers or filters but ionizers that actually emit negative ions. In doing so, they trap dust, which falls to the ground near the ionizer, dirtying the floor but cleaning the air. More importantly they charge the air you breathe back to its natural, ionic state.

Ionizers can work. They do not get you high in the standard sense of the word, but they may make you feel better. Thus they add to the overall high of life. If you do the other exercises in this book indoors—especially those that involve breathing—you should purchase an ionizer to get the maximum effect. There are hundreds on the market now, so you will have to use your judgment in picking out a good one. Among the factors to check are whether or not you have to replace parts, how much air the ionizer can handle per hour, warranties, and price. Read the literature accompanying the particular unit. You should be able to get a sense of the company's priorities. The best units we know of are made by very small companies—usually one or two people—who care enough about their product to put their home phone numbers on the instructions in case you have any problems.

5
SEX

Good sex may be the most intense alteration of consciousness naturally available to earth creatures. The sex act, through a kind of static electricity charged by friction, opposition, and attraction, literally creates the spark of life. Inseparable from this event is the experience of sex itself: a shedding of social values, increased intimacy, vulnerability, total honesty, and a moment of bliss, followed by an alteration of consciousness. This is the mystic experience.

We lose the ability to experience sex fully in several ways. First, we concentrate too much on our sex organs and not enough on our total being. Reducing sex to the "contact of genitals" would be like reducing the experience of an ice cream soda to sucking through a straw. There's a lot more going on than that. We also limit our sexual experience because we are afraid to feel. If you are not in touch with your feelings during the day, you can't expect to suddenly let loose all your passion on cue. To experience sensuous, unafraid sex, you must learn to experience life in a boldly sensuous way. But the biggest obstacle to transcendental sex, and the one really underlying all the others, is a sense of unworthiness.

We limit the possible joy of our sexual encounters because we feel we are not worthy of such an experience. This manifests itself in several ways. A man may think the woman's depth of passion is far greater than his own. He could never please her. He manifests this mind-set in premature ejaculation. On the other hand this same sense of unworthiness could cause him to be a brutish, uncaring lover. He assumes that if he tried to please her, he would fail and he resents his partner for this. The object of his game becomes to please himself while not pleasing her. Similarly a woman's feeling of unworthiness may manifest itself in the belief that the act of sex is for the man's enjoyment and not her own, because she is unworthy of an orgasm. Rather than make her needs known, she "puts up" with sex. Meanwhile all she does is create resentment

in her partner, who can't understand why she isn't satisfied.

Another way we manifest feelings of unworthiness
during sex is by playing "Can you top this?" Couples
strive for more intense orgasms through the use of leather,
whips, and so forth, convinced that they are incapable of
transcendental sex on their own. They are addicted to
orgasm and believe its source is somewhere other than in
the interaction between them.

Before we get too down on ourselves, remember this:
Most people don't have good sex, even if they talk as if
they do. Chances are, the more they boast, the more they
are really just compensating for the shallowness of their
experience. Best of all, the good news is here—it's actually
been here for a dozen or so centuries. For partners or even
solo artists willing to accept the fact that sex is more than
a bump and a squirt, an unlimited range of transcendental
experiences awaits you.

Some final words about this chapter. First, everything
is expressed in terms of male/female energies. This is
because the Taoist and tantric texts are based on that
particular permutation. We assume you can translate most
of these principles to gay and lesbian sex, or any other
kind we might be overlooking. The following techniques
might seem extremely technical, and some of them are.
But even mastery of all the physical techniques in the

world could never truly enhance sex without love. It has always been our opinion that the primary component of good sex is love. Sex is transcendent only when the desire to express love and create pleasure is greater than could possibly be manifest on this plane of existence. It's transcendent because it has to be. Sex is an act of adoration. Even masturbation requires true self-love to be a transcendent act. If you believe that sex and love are two different things and have a stake in that belief structure, try a different chapter.

THE TAO OF SEX

The Tao of sex is based on the same principles as the Tao of anything. Briefly it is that everything manifesting itself on earth is some combination of the two essential forces, yin and yang. Yin is the feminine energy and corresponds with the moon, the night, the earth, while yang is the masculine energy and corresponds with the sun, the day, and the sky. The familiar yin/yang symbol indicates that these two forces are continuously moving, even dancing with each other. The only constant is their circular movement and change. The fuel for this movement is life energy, or *chi*.

The Tao of sex concerns itself with balancing the male

and female energies. Sex becomes a living, working example of the yin/yang in action. The better a couple learns to circulate *chi,* the more nourished they are by each other's energies, the more "electricity" they create, and the more heightened their level of consciousness becomes. The principles for attaining better circulation of *chi* during sex are pretty simple:

1. Ejaculation is not the highest sexual pleasure for a man. In fact the Taoists believed that a man should not ejaculate but once in five or ten sessions. The semen is to be considered an essential and precious life fluid. The older a man is, the more he should retain it. Ejaculation is also something that should never be forced. One need not "change gears" toward the end of a session in order to move towards orgasm. When the body needs to release semen, it will do so.

In practical terms the idea would be for the man to take pleasure in the moment he is in rather than to orient himself toward the goal of orgasm. If he can resist the temptation to move toward orgasm, or learn to control it when the opportunity presents itself, he will reach new heights of sexual bliss. As in any meditative or physical discipline, it is in the moment after you push yourself one step farther that your consciousness goes one level higher.

Prolonged lovemaking may seem difficult at first,

especially for men who equate sex with ejaculation, or have gotten used to a quickie to help them fall asleep. The techniques for delaying orgasm are simple. The easiest, called the locking method, is simply to withdraw the penis whenever the urge to ejaculate occurs. Wait until the urge subsides, then enter again. Another, called the squeeze technique, is also simple. When the man feels the urge to ejaculate, he firmly presses the point between his scrotum and anus. Another method, although not Taoist in origin, is for the man to tell the woman when the urge to ejaculate has come. She, in the straddling position above him, must lift herself off him and squeeze the penis with her thumb and forefinger, just below the tip. When his erection begins to subside, she should mount again.

Prolonged lovemaking, as far as we're concerned, is anything over twenty minutes. But allowing yourself to go for two or three hours can lead to ecstasies beyond what you may have thought were possible.

2. Together with, and even as a result of, the man's retention of semen is an increased focus on the woman's satisfaction. She should be allowed to come to orgasm as much as she wishes. Also, as the "house" of the sexual energy, she is the focus of the sexual act. (This also helps get attention off the penis and ejaculation.) Taoist doctors went through great pains to determine the various physical signs a woman makes to indicate her state of arousal.

We think most receptive lovers can figure this out for themselves. Then, if a woman still isn't getting exactly the kind of arousal she needs—be it harder thrusts or whatever—she can simply ask verbally. Talking during sex is an excellent means of communication.

3. Thrusting techniques are the staple of a Taoist lover's diet. They are described at length in various texts, in terms of both depth and motion. Most popular is the nine-shallow one-deep method, which involves nine shallow thrusts followed by one deep thrust, and then repeats. You can also try five shallow and one deep, or even two shallow and one deep if it doesn't excite uncontrolled ejaculation. As far as the quality of motion is concerned, *The Tao of Love and Sex* by Jolan Chang, has some excellent translations from the *T'ung Hsuan Tzu,* by seventeenth-century physician Li T'ung Hsuan. He uses imagery to describe different thrusting techniques. For example, in one image he instructs the man to see his penis as a warrior striking out to the left and right as if separating the enemy ranks. In another he suggests moving in slowly like a snake sliding into its hole before hibernating. Or, like an eagle attacking its prey, to poise and then dive. A more advanced stroke imitates a sparrow eating rice from a bowl: The man alternates quickly between deep thrusts and light, teasing pecks. You can try thrusting up and down like a wild horse in the rapids, or if this is too

rapid, like a large sailboat in a storm. Vary thrusts to prolong excitation over long periods of lovemaking or to ward off ejaculation.

4. The Taoists are also very concerned with the vital fluids. Saliva, vaginal secretions, and semen all contain vital life energy. In kissing, the couple should try to exchange saliva ("jade fluid"). The woman's yin will be nourished by the man's yang fluids, and vice versa. They also consider a woman's vaginal fluid ("yin essence") to be a vital nutrient for balancing a man's yang energy.

5. The Taoists list too many positions for us possibly to begin listing here. Let it suffice to say they believe in doing it lying down, side to side, sitting up, woman on top, man on top, standing up, from behind—they even describe positions using small mirrors so that lovers can watch their expressions as they move through the various stages of ecstasy. Chances are you can find most of these positions yourselves; referring to diagrams during love-making is decidedly unspontaneous. Remember that variety is the key and that the positions you feel uncomfortable about trying may be just the ones that open new doors.

TANTRIC SEX AND YOGA

Tantric sex is based on the idea that life energy originates at the base of the spine and in the genitals. Sex provides a channel for that energy. The object, though, is not simply to expel the life energy through the sex organs but to help it move up through the various chakras. Most people have experienced a feeling of heat emanating from the middle of their chest during sex. Westerners associate this as love emanating from the heart. According to tantra, this is one of the channels through which the sexual fire flows.

To pursue tantra, watch for workshops being offered in your area, or read *Sexual Secrets: The Alchemy of Ecstasy* by Nik Douglas and Penny Slinger, or the more general treatment in Marcus Allen's *Tantra for the West*. Following are some of the basic tantric beliefs, as well as some things to try at home.

PREPARATION
Preparation, both mental and spiritual, is essential for transcendental sex. Meditate calmly before sex, visualizing (in whatever way you wish) your sexual energy rising from your spine and genitals through your chakras and out the top of your head. Also meditate on your lover as a deity whom you are about to worship through the sex act.

To prepare physically, do some simple yoga asanas. If you are in proper physical condition and have no back problems, try doing a headstand or shoulder stand (against a wall if necessary) and concentrate on the energy flowing downward toward your head. You might also try the cobra position (see chapter 7) with your mouth wide open and your tongue sticking out and down.

SEX AS PRAYER

The tantric texts usually describe making love from the point of view of a yogi praying to his goddess. The sex act is an act of devotion to the Goddess, who is embodied in the female partner, or yogini. Except in moments of supreme ecstasy, when concentration is impossible, the yogi is completely focused on pleasing his lover. Making love is a moving prayer, an offering to the insatiable female deity.

The woman's role is surprisingly similar. She, too, is to find her ecstasy in serving her partner. The best way for her to do this is to allow herself to be consumed by her passion. She mustn't hold back. Tantra accepts the fact that the male and female response curves are different and calls for the yogini to abandon any of her obstacles to letting go. She does this for the sake of the yogi, who is dependent on her release for his own. To sum up, both the man and the woman are focused on *her* pleasure. He strives to give her joy, and she, in receiving it as fully as she can, gives the man his pleasure.

The tantric path to ecstasy is really a manipulation of the orgasm curves of the two partners. Almost like tacking a sailboat back and forth to go in the desired direction, the couple uses each partner's rise and fall to move two steps forward, one step back. The process is actually pretty simple to understand, even if it requires a good deal of stamina to execute. If you have a willing partner and a good few hours, try this one.

The only necessary techniques are the man's abilities to control himself and the woman's ability to release. The tantric techniques for control include most of the ones listed above in Taoist sex. They also suggest concentrating on the sensations in the whole body rather than just the genitals. Imagine energy flowing up through your spine and out the top of your head. To help this energy flow, try rolling your eyes up (don't strain). The focus is on raising the energy up. It is also important for the man to realize it is not he alone who is investing energy into the sex act. Making love (when it is more than coital masturbation) is about a flow of energy, not just a release. True love is not something you spend or something you get. It is at once a circulation of energy and an equilibrium. For both partners steady breathing is a must. For the man it will allow him to regulate his potentially spasmodic body functions.

For the woman, it will keep her from bearing down or holding on.

The tantrics call this sexual technique "Riding the Wave of Ecstasy." There's a complex description of how this works in *Sexual Secrets*, but the basic idea is pretty simple. It's just a matter of alternating between excitor and excitee. After a good period of foreplay and mutual excitation, you begin to have sex. Both focus attention on the woman's pleasure. As the woman reaches her first climax, the man holds back his own. He absorbs the energy released by her orgasm, and as soon as her excitement begins to subside, he brings her back up again. Once she is again moving up, the couple rise together. Now it is the man's turn to approach climax, but just as he gets close to the point of no return, the woman draws him up into the next realm of excitement. (Were she to climax at this point, she would not have the energy to bring him up.) Now it's the man's turn to refrain, then the woman's, then the man's again. The key exchange in this process occurs at the moment the excitor becomes the excitee, just after orgasm or energy leap. You go through this process four times, counting by the woman's orgasms. Each female climax brings the couple to a new chakra. By the fourth one we are in the throat/head area, and the bliss is unreal. You can forget about the techniques now. Climaxes blend into climaxes, even partner blends into partner. Self-consciousness dissolves as both lovers are absorbed into the ecstasy they have created together.

SOMETHING A LITTLE EASIER, PERHAPS

One can experiment with the tantric energies without having sex. Our friend, Jerry, tried this exercise with a woman in his kundalini class and for weeks was convinced he was in love with her. Actually what the yoga process made available to him was a direct experience of the depth from which he could give and receive love and life energy.

The objective of this practice is to circulate energy. First, do a few yoga postures separately from your partner, concentrating on raising your own level of energy. End these individual warm-ups with a more vigorous motion. When you are ready to begin, sit cross-legged facing each other and hold your hands up, palms facing your partner's, pattycake-style but not touching. Leave them about six inches apart and look into your partner's eyes, or up at his or her third eye (between the eyebrows), just so long as you're both doing the same thing. Now imagine a circle of energy flowing from the base of your spine and out through your hands to your partner. Stay like this for at least ten minutes, using your own and your partner's chakrik energies to keep your hands up when they get tired. If your mind drifts, just bring it back to sending as much energy as you can to the other person through the third eye or the hands. You may also begin to experience other connective energies with your partner along various chakras, creating a feeling of warmth at the solar plexus, throat, or lower abdomen.

Next, without breaking the energy fields you've created, and keeping your hands the same distance apart, very slowly move them in small circles, as if wiping steam off a piece of glass between you and your partner. This will feel something like a mirror game. Whenever you get out of synch and the distance between the hands changes, you should feel a strange magnetic tug pulling them back together again.

After you've done this a few minutes, start to play with the energy field you've created. Try pulling your hands slowly apart from those of your partner, or closer to them. Try leaning in with your body, too, and then out. We know people who have used this exercise as a seduction technique, and it probably works as one, but those who use it that way will certainly miss the real joy of this tantric practice.

ORGASM AS BLISS

For all the orgasm retention we've been talking about in this chapter, one would think that it was an unpleasurable experience. Clearly it is not. There are a few simple techniques you can develop in order to experience fuller, more crashing orgasms that create ecstasy for the body, mind, and spirit all at once.

The first is diaphragmatic breathing. Most of us unconsciously hold our breath during difficult or stressful activities. This sets off a chain of physical and mental responses that remove us from the direct experience of whatever we're doing. If you see a gun or firecracker about to go off, your reaction will be to hold your breath, squint, and tense up. To experience full orgasm, you must learn to let go of these reflexes, which are largely anticipatory in nature and deny the joy of a given moment. The orgasm will come in its own time. The more you try to help it along, the less of it there will be when it arrives.

To practice breathing from the diaphragm, lie on your back and relax. Watch the air go in and out. As you inhale, your abdomen should expand, not contract. As you exhale, the abdomen collapses. After you've got this down, you can try to experience the expansion of your back lower ribs as you breathe, then your whole lower back down to your anus, all breathing with you.

Try breathing this way until you've settled into a rhythm and relaxed your entire body. Then let your partner masturbate you or perform oral sex on you. The partner should start by gently caressing other parts of you, slowly working toward your genitals. Intercourse is too advanced for this stage of the game. If you like, you can do this to yourself without a partner, keeping your masturbating hand as relaxed as possible throughout this process. Massage oils and lotions work well for this. As your excitation increases, you may add some sound to your exhalations. A *huh* sound produced from your lower abdomen works well. Throughout all this the key is not to tense up anywhere. Places to watch are your anus, shoulders, neck, hands, and feet. Stay completely relaxed. Most of all do not help in any way, or move yourself toward orgasm consciously. Don't even worry about acknowledging your partner now, if you have a partner. There's time for that later. Just breathe.

As orgasm approaches, the temptation to hold on to your breath or a part of your body will become greater. Use your exhalations and sound to dissipate this need, especially during the orgasm itself. After it's over, follow through by staying absolutely relaxed and breathing diaphragmatically. You will be in physical bliss *and* a highly altered state of consciousness for quite a while.

This is a relatively easy method for achieving an amazing high, and it's as accessible as your hands or your lover. For more advanced techniques, as well as a whole program designed to enhance sexual response and orgasm, see *Total Orgasm* by Jack Lee Rosenberg.

6

EFFORTLESS HIGHS: MEDITATION

Sooner or later most people in search of higher consciousness turn to meditation. While it is probably the most subtle of the methods available to you, it is also the most effective and long-lasting. Unlike skydiving, cassettes, or isolation tanks, meditation is essentially propless. It can be done anywhere, at almost any time. These facts have made meditation our practice of choice.

First, because meditation requires no paraphernalia, you are completely responsible for your experience. Propped highs, such as those derived from mind machines, lead you to identify your pleasurable state of mind with a given machine. In reality the machine is not the experience, any more than a car is the experience of a road trip.

With meditation the illusion of reliance on something outside yourself is much less of a factor. In this way it is the farthest of these techniques from drugs, which create a very strong mind-set of dependence. Meditation, simply put, is choosing to get high and then doing so. No tricks, no gimmicks, no effort. This is probably why it is so hard for Westerners to believe it works. "I don't have to *do* anything?" Nope. In fact the knack of meditation, if there is one, is learning how to do nothing—or, if you must do something, watching yourself doing it rather than getting caught up in results or judgments. Western thought dictates that effort leads to results. While this may be true for industry or even weight lifting, it is not true for getting high through meditation.

Your Western goal orientation can be exploited during the first stages of meditation, though, so don't worry too much about it. If you are meditating "in order to get high," that's okay. As you meditate, your goal will probably vanish before your eyes. You'll be in a state of bliss where reaching toward fun or anything other than where you are will seem a worthless, off-centering effort. Getting started in meditation for a specific reason is fine. Just be willing to watch that reason change if it wants to.

The "reasons" to meditate are your mind's way of permitting the activity. The receptionist needs to feel justified in putting this on your daily calendar. Let the following suffice: Meditation improves physical health by slowing your pulse, lowering your blood pressure, deepening your respiration, improving your vision as well as your other senses, and regulating the function of nearly all your organs and glands. It improves your mental health by reducing stress, improving concentration, dissipating neuroses, providing deep relaxation, curtailing depression, augmenting synaptic transmission, and making you smarter, calmer, and quicker. Meditation also feels good, gets you high, leads to spiritual advancement, and might even bring you toward enlightenment.

The way meditation works is rather simple. It takes your consciousness past the receptionist and out of the office for a while. There are two ways of getting beyond the receptionist's control: Get it busy or put it to sleep. Then you can walk right past it and outside. You don't even have to sneak. Float right up and out through the ceiling if you feel like it. There are no longer any rules. The methods of getting the mind occupied are varied. Some involve chanting a mantra, focusing on an object such as a candle, or even trying to work out a complex problem or paradox. Putting the mind to sleep is simple: Watch it for long enough and it will just konk out.

Whenever the mind presents you with an issue or problem during your meditation, simply nod and say, "That's nice," or "That's thinking." Keep doing that, not allowing your consciousness to attach to any of the thoughts that arise, and you will soon move to a place far beyond the plane of thought.

In this chapter we have outlined a good number of meditative techniques. The one you choose is unimportant. Do whatever sounds best to you. This chapter is dedicated to still meditations. All you need to do is sit down somewhere and begin. In the next chapter we outline moving meditations, which involve either a simple or a complex motion of the body.

There are four main meditative paths. One appeals to the intellect and is called contemplation. Rather than escaping from the mind, you occupy it with your own agenda. The mind then assists your ascent. Another path is through the emotions. Through devotion to God or a master you experience perfect love. You see how the object of your devotion is perfection. Slowly you are able to apply this vision of perfection to the entire universe, including yourself. Mantra meditation involves the repetition of a word or phrase, either vocally or mentally. The sound acts as a vehicle for your consciousness to travel to new places. There are also a great variety of unstructured meditations, ranging from simple mindfulness to thinking about a particular problem. The final goal of all of these processes is to bring the meditative state into your daily awareness. Life itself becomes a meditation. You are always conscious, always high.

To prepare for meditation, you need to do a few things. First, make sure you are in satisfactory physical condition. Meditation involves sitting still for long periods of time, sometimes on the floor or on a meditation pillow. Yoga (described in the next chapter) was invented to prepare the body for meditation. You might want to do several weeks of asanas (exercises) before beginning, or do them before each time you meditate. Any of the techniques outlined here can also be done in a good chair that keeps your back straight.

JUST DO IT

Regularity is important. You should meditate at least once a day, and at the same time each day. It takes about a month for any activity to become habitual, and you want meditation to become a part of your life. It's time to quit window shopping, sit down, and commit to the quality of your life experience. You are not "spending" an hour of your day. You are "getting" an hour of what life is about. You deserve it. When you don't feel like meditating, realize that this is your mind coming up with an excuse to leave things as they are. Meditation is not hard. Sitting down for an hour (or even twenty minutes) is hardly an act of great discipline, although the mind will convince you that it is, or that meditation is painfully boring. It is not. An hour of television is boring. Soaring outside the boundaries of time and space is thrilling. Believe us, it works.

Another way to create regularity is to meditate with a group or class. Having other people meditating around you helps reinforce the notion that what you're doing is good. It also makes it harder to get up and quit. A group meditation creates a field of energy in which it is easier for each meditator to break away from normal consciousness.

We also suggest that you set aside a place in your house or apartment where you only meditate. You don't need to build an altar or invest in a Japanese bonsai garden. You might want to buy a meditation pillow or some incense and establish one corner of a room as your meditation space. You may hang a particularly inspiring photo or painting in this place. Creating a meditation space not only gives you a place to call home, it also helps you feel more committed to your practices.

When doing almost any meditation, you will get an urge to stop. You might feel bored or impatient, or suddenly remember something you had to do or someone you had to call. Tough. Sit it out. Almost as soon as you let those thoughts pass and recommit to your meditation, fantastic new depths are reached. It's like a spiritual second wind. The way to push over these humps of resistance is by *not* pushing. Do not force yourself to stay in meditation. Rather relax farther into the meditation. Exhale deeply, feel your forehead relax, and begin your particular mantra, thought, or technique again.

This cycle—meditation leading to miscellaneous thought leading to boredom or impatience and then back into deeper meditation—is the process by which you move into fuller states of consciousness. You are not just going in circles but rather ascending a spiral staircase, where each successive step corresponds to a step directly beneath itself. It may seem as if you are in the same place as before, but you are actually one level higher.

So, remove all your expectations, read through the following techniques, pick one, and go for it. If you prefer to work with a teacher or meditation group, look in your local yellow pages under "Meditation Instruction" or purchase a copy of *Meditation* magazine, which has a large listing of meditation schools and groups in the back. Ram Dass's book *Journey of Awakening* dedicates over a hundred pages to a directory of retreat facilities and groups that teach meditation.

SIMPLE MEDITATIONS

WATCHING THE BREATH

The simplest meditation is to watch your breath. All you need to do is find a comfortable, upright sitting position, either on the floor, on a pillow, or in a chair. Close your eyes and begin to notice the breath passing in and out of your nostrils. Your mind will invariably wander, but as you notice yourself thinking about something other than the breath, gently bring your attention back to the sensation of the air passing through your nose.

CANDLE MEDITATIONS

This process is the same as the breathing meditation, but instead of focusing on the breath you focus on a candle flame. Place a candle a foot or so in front of you and just look at it. Again, as you notice the mind wandering, gently bring your awareness back to the flame. This meditation is slightly more difficult, because it requires a greater effort at focusing your mind on a single point.

TWO ROCKS

This one of the most powerful meditations we have tried, and it is quite easy. Find two rocks of different weights. Stand or sit with one rock in each hand and close your eyes. Move your hands around gently as you concentrate on balancing the two stones. Make them weigh the same. This sounds absurd at first, but treat it like a mind game if you must. Soon you will begin to notice that the rocks do seem to change their relative weights. Once the rocks seem to weigh the same, exchange one for the other and rebalance them in the opposite hands. Do this three or four times. It should take anywhere from twenty minutes to an hour. The meditation works by bringing your consciousness to a place where the energy of the earth, gravity, no longer rules. You are free of the laws that hold you down on the ground.

THIRD EYE

The third eye is a point on your lower forehead, just above where your eyebrows would meet. This point is used in many Indian meditations, as well as this one. Third-eye meditations are the most noticeably transcendental for us. We often feel quite altered for several hours afterward.

For this meditation find a tree and sit or stand five to fifteen feet away from it, depending on its size and how you feel. Imagine a silver thread connecting your third eye with a specific point on the bark of the tree. Concentrate on that point on the bark and your connection to it. Do this for forty-five minutes. Two variations on this meditation involve chanting the sound *OM*. If you are seated, simply chant the sound, one long *OOOOMMMM* on each exhalation. If you are standing, do the same chant, but also slowly step three or four steps toward, then three or four steps away from, the tree as you breathe and chant. Your arms should be at your sides, with your palms facing back.

THE SUBLIME

The next time you are in a truly beautiful place, such as a mountain range or waterfall, try this simple practice. Sit somewhere comfortable, facing the most majestic vista you can find. For example, face the peak of a mountain or the top of a waterfall. Put your wrists on your knees and gently tap your index finger and thumb together, once a second or more. During this, as slowly as you can, open and close your eyes repeatedly. The process of getting your eyes open should take thirty seconds or so, and after they are completely open, you should begin to close them again, in a controlled movement taking just as much time. Do this for at least fifteen minutes.

ORIENTAL PATHS

BUDDHISM

The Buddhists have developed some of the least "religious"-seeming meditations. They often involve no mantras, statues, or specific ideology. Here is one of the basic techniques of the Buddhists called Vipassang and probably the most likely sort you will encounter if you seek out a Buddhist meditation center. It is the primary practice of Theravaddin Buddhism, but has been adopted as a preliminary practice by many other sects as well.

The rules are simple; the practice is less so. All you do is sit, breathe, and watch thoughts go by. As soon as you realize you are having a thought, label it "thinking." You may use the word *thinking* if you like, or just acknowledge that you had a thought and move on. To refocus, concentrate on your exhalation. If you are distracted by a sound or body sensation, do the same thing: Return to watching your breath. You should breathe through both mouth and nose. Don't try to control the breath; just watch it. Experience the sensation of it exiting your mouth. Once you have recentered, you can let consciousness of your breathing fade away. Do this in a seated position, with your eyes open, for at least thirty minutes to start. Although your eyes are open, you aren't looking at anything in particular. You should let your eyes rest on an area of the floor five or six feet in front of you.

Another form of this meditation alternates between the above technique and a walking meditation. Do the sitting meditation for forty-five minutes, then, for fifteen minutes, walk around the room or garden, concentrating on the sensation of the soles of your feet against the floor instead of your outgoing breath. Your head should be down, and your hands clasped in the following manner: The left hand is curled into a light fist, with the thumb on top, while the right hand clasps the left wrist, so that the right thumb can rest in the space between your left thumb and the knuckle of your left index finger. Place your hands in this position on your navel and walk. Again, whenever a thought comes into your consciousness, label it "thinking" and return your awareness to the sensation of your feet against the floor. After fifteen minutes of this, go back to the sitting meditation again.

This meditation opens up your awareness to the space between your thoughts. Often we believe that we *are* our thoughts; this is not true. Our consciousness is a continuum into which individual thoughts may penetrate, like the ticks of a clock into the silence around them. This silence, this peace, is the state of pure awareness.

THE HINDUS

BHAKTI

Although it seems somewhat inaccessible to Westerners, Bhakti meditation is worthy of mention here, if for no other reason than that it is the principal form of prayer in

Hinduism. It is a devotional practice in which the meditator concentrates on an inspiring god or guru. By devoting your entire thought and energy to the *ishta*, as the object of devotion is called, you can free yourself of all other, worldly attachments. You are eventually able to see the perfection, or God, in all things and people, even yourself. This is the way many Christian churches work. Through complete devotion to Jesus, one is enabled to see the Jesus in all creation.

Bhakti practice consists of chanting something like "Hare Krishna, Hare Krishna, Krishna Krishna, Hare Hare. Hare Rama, Hare Rama, Rama Rama, Hare Hare." Hare, Rama, and Krishna are three names for the Lord. *Hare* means "the one who steals our heart"; *Rama* means "the one who fills us with joy"; *Krishna* means "the one who draws us to him." If you're not afraid of cultish behavior, visit your local Hare Krishna center on a Sunday afternoon and try taking part in their devotional singing and dancing.

The interesting thing about devotional highs is that they take into account the fact that highs often seem to come from an external source, such as a mantra. These practices exploit our sense of unworthiness and our belief system so that we are incapable of manifesting higher consciousness on our own. The devotee identifies all positive experience with the *ishta*. Only later is the practitioner able to feel the *ishta* within.

Still, devotion is an excellent high, as long as you feel secure that the object of your devotion won't turn on you or prove somehow unworthy, as many Christian evangelists have recently. Devotional activities also include charity work, such as cooking food at a shelter for the homeless or donating time to the Red Cross. Whether or not these activities can be called meditations is debatable. The idea here would be to keep in mind as you work that your whole being is dedicated to serving God, the deity in others, and the holiness in yourself.

KUNDALINI

Kundalini is a kick-ass form of Hindu meditation and yoga. The yoga postures and movements are discussed in the next chapter, but should be done in combination with the meditation techniques outlined here. The kundalini system is the most well researched of the Hindus and bases all of its practices on an intricate system of chakras, breathing, astrology, and brain patterns. The belief is that life energy begins at the base of the spine, then moves up through the various chakras, past the open window of the third eye, and out through the last chakra on the crown of the skull. Whether or not the kundalini model is exactly accurate, be forewarned: These meditations are very powerful. They involve manipulation of energies from deep within you and can produce some shocking states of consciousness, from euphoria to out-of-body travel. Thus it is advisable to find a kundalini teacher if you choose to pursue this deeply. You can contact the Kundalini Research Institute at 800 North Park Avenue, Suite 5, Pomona, California 91768, or the 3HO Foundation, International Headquarters, House of Guru Ram Dass, 1620 Preuss Road, Los Angeles, California 90035.

Usually a kundalini session would consist of physical exercise followed by meditation. After that the meditator takes time to experience a deep relaxation. Group songs usually follow, and then a prayer ends the event.

SAH TAH NAH MAH

This is one of the first meditations a kundalini student learns. Sit on a pillow or on the floor and close your eyes. Concentrate on the third eye as you slowly chant the sounds *SAH TAH NAH MAH*. Use the melody of the first four notes of "Mary Had a Little Lamb" (MA-RY HAD A . . .) Begin by chanting in a normal voice. After five minutes, go into a whisper. Then, after another five minutes, do the mantra mentally. As you chant each syllable, gently tap each of your fingers against your thumbs. The index fingers on *SAH*, the middle fingers on

TAH, the ring finger on *NAH*, and the pinkie on *MAH*, then repeat.

If you have trouble concentrating or experience any uncomfortable physical symptoms during the meditation, focus on each sound of the mantra passing down through the opening on the crown of your skull and out again through your third eye. When you are finished, gently stretch before opening your eyes.

SAT NAM

This mantra is an abbreviated form of *SAH TAH NAH MAH*. We include this meditation because the first time our friend, Steve, tried it, he went out-of-body. Needless to say, he was on a relaxed high for a week or so afterward. Again, if this works for you, please seek out a qualified kundalini yoga teacher. If these exercises are to be done every day, they should be done correctly and as part of a planned program. Also, these exercises might be injurious to anyone who has back or other physical problems. Consult a doctor about the appropriateness of these exercises for you before attempting to do any position described here or by a yoga teacher.

The exercise is in several parts:

First, sit cross-legged and inhale through puckered lips to make a whistling sound, exhaling through your nose. As you inhale, imagine the sound reverberating at your third eye. Do this for several minutes.

Then change your breathing so that you inhale through your nose and exhale, whistling, through puckered lips. On inhaling, think of the sound *SAT* and on exhaling think of the sound *NAM*.

After doing that for several minutes lie down on your stomach, put your palms on the floor next to your chest, and push up, gently arching your back. (This is not a push-up. Do not pivot at the feet. Leave your thighs on the floor, arching your back—don't push it. Remember, you should only be doing this with the permission of your doctor and under the supervision of a qualified instructor.) Stare at a point on the ceiling directly above you. This is called the cobra position. This should tire you out within a couple of minutes. Don't push beyond your ability. Exhale, and roll onto your back. Close your eyes. Pull your knees into your chest and clasp your arms around them. This pulls your spine into the opposite curve. Pull your head up between your knees and chant the sound *NNNNNNNNN*.

When you get tired, rest by lying on your back and crossing your legs. The legs are crossed as if you were sitting up Indian-style. This straightens out the spine.

When you are ready, sit cross-legged. Put your hands on your shoulders, thumbs behind and fingers in front.

Swivel your torso, leading with your elbows, left and right, like the inside of a washing machine. As with this entire exercise, care must be taken not to strain or injure the spine. Inhale as you go left and exhale as you go right. After a minute or so, sit on your heels, with your knees on the floor in front of you. After a minute of this, take one last deep inhalation, hold it, then exhale deeply.

To end this meditation, relax by leaning forward over your knees. Allow your hands to slide back toward your feet, palms up. Relax as much as you can.

THE RELAXATIONS

It is in the final relaxation that you feel the full effects of these meditations. After either one of these meditations, try a slow mantra *SAH TAH NAH MAH* four times as you inhale slowly through your nose and hold your in breath long enough to complete the four repetitions. Exhale more quickly, and with a little sound of air against your lips, as you imagine the faster mantra *WUH GROO*. Your mind may wander from the mantra and breathing technique, so if you realize this is happening, bring yourself back to the practice.

We can't overemphasize how powerful this technique can be. When you are finished, it might be a good idea to hum a little tune or random notes to yourself before opening your eyes. We also suggest gentle stretching before you try to stand.

THE KABBALAH

Kabbalah is the much-misunderstood and much-underestimated mystical branch of Judaism. Do not expect to learn much about it at most synagogues. While Judaism, because of the way it is popularly conceived, is not the first place most people turn in order to find transcendental meditation techniques, those who do are often surprised by how much Jewish mystics understood about states of consciousness.

SHIN MEM MEDITATION

This is a short, easy meditation with quickly observed effects. You alternate between making the sound *SHHHH* and making the sound *MMMMM*. Make one sound for fifteen or twenty seconds, then switch to the other. What this meditation does is to tune your consciousness alternately to the chaotic white noise of *shh* and the higher, focused, and directed sound of *MMM*. The Kabbalistic tradition states that the way to higher consciousness involves just briefly experiencing higher states so that they can be readily integrated into normal life. You only need to do this meditation for a couple of minutes.

ALPHABET SOUP

In *Path of the Kabbalah* David Shienkin outlines an ancient meditation technique based on the Hebrew alphabet. The letters of the Hebrew alphabet are thought to be more than just representations of sounds; they are mystical symbols. Each has its own special resonance. All you have to do is pick a letter (any Hebrew text or lesson book should have them all). Stare at the letter and meditate on its shape. Once you have the letter committed to memory, close your eyes and continue to visualize it. Another form of meditation is to imagine sculpting or chiseling the letter out of stone. Keep sculpting until only the letter remains in blank space. The most difficult of the techniques is to attempt to imagine the letter as black fire and the background behind it as white fire.

If these techniques resonate for you, contact a Kabbalistic institute, if you can find one. There are places to learn in New York and Los Angeles. Otherwise find some good books and translations and explore it yourself. The Jews spent hundreds of years traveling with books and no teachers, but managed to do a pretty good job of preserving the mystic texts, even if we have to go digging through the back shelves of bookstores in order to find them.

7
MOVING
MEDITATIONS

Like sitting meditations, moving meditations attempt to free consciousness from the limitations of the mind. Since movements of the body are controlled by the brain, learning new movement patterns retrains neural pathways. For example if you are nervous but engage in calm movements, your mind will settle down. Likewise, if you engage in transcendental movements, you will get high.

Each of the following moving meditations functions in a different way. You should determine with your doctor which of these techniques is appropriate for you and, when you decide, seek out a qualified instructor. T'ai Chi

Chuan is a martial art based on the I Ching and teaches control of *chi* energy through slow, constant movement. Kundalini is a form of yoga that raises energy from the base of the spine through to the higher chakras, transforming lower and sexual energies to mental and spiritual ones. Sufi movement meditations range from sensory awareness to Whirling Dervish dances, which bring the dancer into a state of rapture, one with God. Feldenkrais is the father of modern movement-awareness techniques, which enhance movement through expanded consciousness and widen consciousness through better movement.

As with any technique outlined in this book, you should consult a doctor to make sure you are sufficiently physically fit to try any particular exercises. In giving these warnings, we are reminded of the time a student approached his T'ai Chi instructor and asked, "My knee hurts when I move it like this. What should I do?" To which the teacher calmly replied, "Don't move it like that."

T'AI CHI CHUAN

T'ai Chi Chuan is the first and best martial art. Having studied it for the past six years, we admit we've somewhat biased in its favor, but the fact remains that this ancient martial-arts movement technique provides the basis for all the other martial arts. If you are interested in studying martial arts, begin with T'ai Chi. If you are not interested in studying martial arts, T'ai Chi is also excellent for the health of internal organs, regulation and improved awareness of the flow of *chi* energy throughout the body, increased intuitive understanding of the I Ching, and better posture, coordination, and endurance.

Most teachers do not teach T'ai Chi as a fighting technique. They teach a "form," consisting of somewhere between 60 and 120 movements, depending upon the style. The individual movements have names such as Carry Tiger to Mountain or Wave Hands Like Clouds. As far as our classmate Morgan was concerned, he was learning an easy, slow, cool-looking dance. One year into his training he was mugged in New York. His hands instantly flew into a movement called White Crane Spreads Its Wings. He had struck his attacker once in the gut with his elbow and again in the face with relaxed fingers before he even realized he was being threatened. He never knew White Crane Spreads Its Wings could be used in that way, and he probably couldn't use it the same way consciously, but he immediately gained new respect for the pretty movements he was practicing.

What keeps Morgan involved in T'ai Chi, however, is the way it makes him feel. Doing the T'ai Chi form is the surest way he knows to get altered positively every time. After two minutes on a good day, or twenty minutes on a bad day, his arms and legs feel weightless as they float through space. His mind is fixed on the motion, which never stops. His hands control a ball of energy, *chi*, that seems to emanate from every part of him. At times he shakes, trembles, cries, or laughs, but he is always left extremely calm, clear-headed, and behaving like the person he always wished he could be.

It is close to impossible to learn T'ai Chi without an instructor. You can't know if you are doing the movements correctly until you understand them as motions and not positions drawn or photographed in a book. T'ai Chi is kinetic, not static. Still, here's an exercise that moves internal energy while leaving the body in one position.

FIRE HORSE

We won't say this isn't a taxing exercise, but the results can be immediate and extraordinary.

You stand with your feet pointing straight ahead, shoulder-width apart or wider. Keeping your back straight, you bend your knees so that they stay in the direction of your feet. (Do not let them buckle in.) You are now in the position of a person riding a horse. You slowly raise your arms in front of you and hold them as if you were carrying a huge beach ball. The arms are rounded, the palms facing you, about eye level. The fingers are spread and pointed toward each other, about six or eight inches apart. The thumbs are on top but curled to point toward each other.

As you stay in this position, you imagine energy flowing out through each of your arms, crossing in front of you through the gap between your hands to circle around your back. You can imagine it as light, water, or anything that works for you. Stare at a point between your fingers on the wall or in the garden in front of you. Now, try to stay in this position for ten to fifteen minutes. This may sound crazy to you, but it's not. It is not an exercise of muscular strength. What keeps the arms up is *chi* energy. What brings them down is lack of concentration on the flow of that energy. We know there will be some difficult moments during this exercise. (Stop if you feel pain.) Your instructor will encourage you to push through them by relaxing further and concentrating more deeply. It is at precisely these moments that you have the opportunity to get very high. Go for it.

KUNDALINI YOGA

Kundalini is also a technique that is best learned from a teacher or in a group practice. This form of yoga deals with very powerful energies, so it's the ideal yoga to use for altering consciousness. The high energies put into play, however, make it all the more important for you to be doing the exercise correctly. If you like the following practice, seek out a qualified teacher before ingraining any bad habits and possibly doing damage to yourself.

The people who practice kundalini yoga are the most intellectual branch of Indian yogis. They have elaborate explanations for how each of the exercises works and they plan long sessions of yoga, meditation, and prayer. They would probably argue that these exercises do not work properly outside the context of a fuller kundalini practice. We have found, though, that even done infrequently these exercises can provide a sense of great alertness and well-being. That alone should help motivate anyone enjoying these techniques to seek out further guidance.

BREATH OF FIRE
This is a basic constituent of many of the kundalini exercises, but can be done independently of them as well. Breath of Fire is a powerful technique. Do this only with

a qualified instructor. You sit comfortably, with your back straight. You then breathe through the nose only, in quick, short contractions. Using your abdomen to control the breath, you simply pull in the navel to expel air, in a sharp, forced exhalation. Repeat this again and again in rapid succession. Relax for an instant between each exhalation and the vacuum you have created will fill up with air naturally. You do not need to inhale consciously. You would do this as rapidly as you can, leaving your whole body relaxed except for your abdomen. You should have a box of tissues nearby, because Breath of Fire tends to clear out your nostrils. Do this for a minute at a time, until you can sustain it for longer. When you are finished, proceed to one of the kundalini meditations.

DERVISHES

The Whirling Dervish dances, developed by the Sufis, produce a state of consciousness unlike any other we have known. They are said to have been invented spontanteously by Sufi saint Jalalu'ddin Rumi in the thirteenth century. He had been mourning the death of his best friend and passed by a goldsmith's shop. He began to chant "Allah" to the rhythm of the goldsmith's pounding hammer and started to spin wildly in the street. The pure ecstasy he is said to have experienced in that moment is what Sufi dancers are reaching for in their spinning.

Unfortunately the Turks made dervish dances illegal for about twenty-five years from 1925 to 1950, so there are few practiced Sufi masters around today teaching this stuff. Contact a Sufi order (through Sufi Order, P.O. Box 396, New Lebanon, New York 12125) if you wish to pursue the theology. They probably won't teach you to dance for a while, though.

The Sufis believe that we are held down by worldly cares, locked into an inferior reality by our lower selves. The only salvation comes through consciousness of God. The hypnotic spinning of the Whirling Dervishes is based on this Sufi doctrine, and leaves the dancer feeling like a pure channel of energy—almost like a tornado: spinning and frictionless, formless, except as an interface between two different fields of psychic pressure. While you cannot try this yourself—spinning is dangerous—you could enter a Sufi school or attend a dervish performance.

We have danced with the dervishes. It happens like this: The dervish puts his arms out to his sides, the right palm facing the sky, and the left palm facing the earth. The dancer imagines energy from God coming down from heaven and into the right palm. The energy passes through his body, initiating a spiraling sensation and passing out through the left palm, down into the earth. The dancer begins to spin in a counterclockwise direction (counterclockwise to a spectator viewing from above). If he is spinning correctly, the dancer will not get dizzy. It is the energy current between the heavens and the earth that maintains his whirling.

JAPANESE ZEN ARCHERY

It would be close to impossible to teach or even fully explain archery in a book, so even if we were Zen-archery masters, which we are not, we wouldn't attempt it here. Kyudo, as it is called in Japanese, is a very focused form of moving meditation that allows the archer to experience the oneness of mind, spirit, and body by practicing to stay exactly in the moment. One of the main ideas here is not to think about hitting the target. The archer concentrates on the form of the movement, which is a set of very discrete positions: raising the bow, raising the arrow, pulling back, and so forth. One does not "shoot" the arrow at the target. The target and arrow are already joined. One releases the arrow and lets it find the center of the target. If it misses the target, it is because the archer got in the way.

    The arrow, bow, and target are indicators of one's inner state. For example, if the arrow wobbles, the archer is wobbly and off-center. In this way, unlike most other moving meditations, you are provided with a barometer of your progress. Almost like a psychic biofeedback machine, archery allows you to experiment with different states of consciousness and directly observe their extension into physical reality.

The best way to begin to learn Zen archery is to take a good weekend or week-long retreat with a master instructor. Courses are listed in New Age or martial arts magazines. The best, most accessible instruction is available year-round at Ryuko Kyudojo (4220 19th Street, Boulder, Colorado 80302).

THE FELDENKRAIS METHOD

Moshe Feldenkrais developed a series of exercises called Awareness Through Movement. Ostensibly it is a system of exercises that improve your ability to move by heightening your awareness of the way the body works. This is not limited to the physical relationship of joints to bones or tendons to muscles. The Feldenkrais method also concerns the relationship of the mind to the body. It is in exploring this interface between intention and movement that these exercises provide access to strange levels of consciousness.

Often a Feldenkrais exercise will begin by testing the range of motion of a certain part of your body. You will then do a simple movement that teaches you how this body part works—not a stretch but an awareness exercise. When you retest the range of motion, you will find that it has greatly increased. Much more astonishing, though, you will learn how to do the exercise mentally—not even moving—and get the same results. If you like the description of the following exercise, you can find a Feldenkrais class in most cities, especially through acting schools. One of the best things about this system is that it is very easy to do, and it provides tangible evidence of its effects.

A FELDENKRAIS EXERCISE

The rule with these exercises is not to push. Nothing in Feldenkrais should ever hurt. You stand comfortably, putting your right arm directly in front of you, parallel to the ground. Begin with a test: You turn your upper torso (including your arm) to the right, seeing how far you can rotate without straining at all. Remember a place on the wall so that you can mark how far you turned. Now the exercise: You gently and slowly move your arm (still parallel to the floor) to the right as you turn your head to the left. You bring them both back to center, and then off to the sides again in unison. Nice and easy. After doing this ten or fifteen times, you retest how far you can rotate to the right. Then you do the same exercise, moving your arm to the right and head to the left, while you keep your eyes fixed on a spot in front of you, causing them to move to the right side of your eye sockets. You retest your rotation and see how much you've improved.

Now the amazing part: Raising your left arm directly in front of you, you test your range of motion in a rotation to the left. Now imagine doing the exercises you actually did with your right arm. First you imagine moving your head to the right and arm to the left fifteen times. Remember the sensation of doing that on the right and translate it to the left. You test your range of motion again. Now imagine doing the second exercise ten or fifteen times (the same as the first, but keeping your eyes fixed forward so that they swing left in the sockets). Again you test your range of motion. It should be just as improved.

This exercise, admittedly, is not enough to get you high, but it does indicate the path of Feldenkrais's work. In the more advanced exercises your mind moves to some pretty bizarre places as your perception of your body changes drastically. It is an intensely physical high, where you become acutely aware of the essence of motion. By exploring the interface between mind and body, you will gain access to a new place in your consciousness.

8

LOOK MA,
NO HANDS!

This is a chapter of rushes. Rushes are the easiest altered state to recognize, but, strictly speaking, they are not highs. A rush is like the feeling you get when you dream that you are falling or flying. Even asleep, you can feel your whole body responding to the fact that you are in flight. Then when you wake up, your heart is pounding and you are exhilarated.

A rush can be thought of as a quick, intense burst of high. The state of consciousness is so heightened that it cannot be sustained for very long. Rushes are the high of choice for our goal-oriented Western culture. Just as we equate education with a diploma and sex with orgasm, we equate fun with "what a rush!" But to keep getting rushes, we feel the need to do increasingly intense or dangerous things.

People become addicted to rushes. Kids in search of cheap thrills try ever-increasingly dangerous activities to get that feeling of excitement. They try everything from doing stunts on their bicycles to stealing things from stores to experimenting with drugs. Eventually they get caught, or hurt—or worse.

Luckily for us, there are other, safer ways of experiencing a rush. None of them need to be truly dangerous in order to work; they merely need to activate our instinctive sense of self-preservation. You can get a great rush simply looking straight down from the top of the World Trade Center. While the activity itself is not dangerous, your *body* doesn't know that. The human body doesn't understand things like plate glass. The body doesn't understand airplanes, or parachutes, or roller coasters or Imax movies. It is your body that we are about to fool.

FALLING

Jung said that we all have dreams about falling or flying. This sensation and rush of adrenaline is, apparently, a natural human discharge. To experience this in the waking state, we have developed several sports and activities that imitate the dream fall. They include roller coasters, down-hill sports, and actual airborne glides, falls, and floats.

SKYDIVING

All we can explain about skydiving in this book is what it feels like. You simply must take a set of lessons with a qualified instructor in order to skydive without dying. They are not very expensive, and if you are somewhat coordinated, you can usually be jumping from an airplane within a couple of days. Of course skydiving can be very dangerous. Before engaging in this activity you should check with your doctor to make sure you're suited to this sport, and then learn the proper techniques from a licensed skydiving school. The difficult things about skydiving are jumping and landing. Once you conquer the instinct that tells you not to jump out of an airplane, you are on your way.

The skydiving high is perfectly structured. It goes something like this: You prepare by checking and rolling up your parachute. You feel an intense appreciation for the craftsmanship that went into this piece of silk, knowing that your life will be depending on it in just a few minutes. Then you step into a small airplane and take off. You sit in this small craft, in full knowledge that this plane exists solely for the purpose of jumping out of it. In fact everyone around you is part of an insane group of people that spend their money and time jumping out of airplanes for fun. Someone might tell a story about "that guy last year whose chute got stuck." Great. After a while everyone gets quiet. The plane just keeps going up and up. And up.

By the time they open the door, all you want to do is go home. You don't care that you've already spent your money on lessons. You just don't want to die. You are persuaded to move toward the door and you look out. You swear this plane is flying higher than any plane you've ever been on. Is the pilot sure he's over the landing spot? It doesn't look familiar.

Then, for some reason, in a moment you can't remember, you jumped from the plane. Just when you decided not to, something inside jumped out and your body followed. Panic. There is no up or down. Everything is moving. You are tumbling. Count. You were supposed to count. You need to be a certain distance from the plane before you pull the cord. Where did everybody go? You want to go home.

Finally you pull your cord and the unexpected happens. You go straight up. You are yanked up like a yo-yo. The rush begins. Your face is somewhere down in your stomach. Your whole body is buzzing. You don't know if it feels good or not. It's just really fast and really weird.

Then at last everything stops. Peace. You look up. The chute is open. You look down—whoops, maybe don't look down, not yet anyway. You notice that you can hear for the first time. The wind rushes in your ears but compared with before, this is heaven. You swing and float, float and swing. You remember to breathe. Except for the heartbeat at your temples, this is bliss. This lasts a good long while.

Soon the ground approaches. It doesn't seem to come that fast. The landing should be easy. You find a nice grassy place, steer the best you can, get ready to bend your legs like the instructor said, and BAM! Ow! Harder than you thought it was going to be, but nothing's broken. You're alive. You just want to sit for a moment and look up.

You just jumped out of an airplane, and for no other reason than to do it.

HANG GLIDING

Like parachuting, hang gliding is a sport in which the realization constantly hits you that you are doing something dangerous for the pure exhilaration of it. In gliding, though, you have a bit more control over your experience. It's a little harder, and somewhat more dangerous, because you usually jump off rocky cliffs rather than into clear air. But you are dependent on your own skill, which for some is a necessary component of a good thrill. In parachuting, you are at the mercy of your rip cord and gravity. In hang gliding (and in the more guided forms of parachuting) you are more the master of your experience. A glide is also a great deal longer than a parachute jump. A jump lasts a couple of minutes. A good glide can last an hour.

Again, this can be an extremely dangerous activity, especially if done without proper supervision and training. The only way to experience hang gliding is by finding a qualified, licensed instructor and of course checking with your doctor to make sure your body can tolerate the kinds of stresses this sport entails. We think the best way to get started gliding is to take a guided tour on a two-person glider. There are a number of instructors who will take passengers on their gliders with them. You pay forty or fifty bucks for a ride of half an hour or so. This is great fun because you don't have the responsibility of steering the contraption, but you get one hell of a ride.

Unlike parachuting, hang gliding is done from a horizontal position. This allows you to look down much more easily. It also makes you feel more like you are flying rather than just falling. You move forward, not just down. Take-off is a little different, too, in that your role is much more active. In hang gliding you must make a running start toward the edge of a cliff, then leap off.

Hang gliding requires a few more lessons than parachuting, but is ultimately cheaper and a little more natural. Once you find a good spot—Aspen has some of the best—you can just bring your glider and go. The scenery is usually a little better, too, because you have mountains around you rather than just open fields. Still, you don't get the exhilaration of free-falling—unless your glider breaks; but then that'll be the end of you.

ROLLER COASTERS

Companies like Six Flags and Disney come out with new rides every year, each designed to disorient you in a new way. Some use water, others use lights, and others even show movies to you as you drop. All of these rides do essentially the same thing: allow you to fall fast. (Always follow instructions.)

Our favorite roller coasters are the ones made out of wood. These are scarier to us for several reasons. First, they make noise. Second, they are not gliding smoothly on metal tracks, but on old wooden slats. At any moment, it seems, something could come loose, and the coaster cars could go careening through the railing and out over the park. Old coasters work by gravity. As in a parachute drop, you experience a slow ascent that builds to a peak, then out of nowhere the great fall begins.

Many metal coasters have more intense drops, or even complete loops, but the experience is different. It feels more controlled. Still, in terms of pure motion, metal coasters provide the most extreme experiences. Six Flags now boasts a coaster (in California it's called Ninja) in which you stand rather than sit. There is a metal loop-de-loop coaster in nearly every American city and numerous small-radius spirals that are possible only on metal coasters.

Disney's Space Mountain is also a pretty intense coaster experience. Space Mountain is a "Space Odyssey"-style roller coaster completely enclosed in a huge dome. It is a roller coaster ride in the dark, with projections of stars and galaxies on the walls and ceiling. What makes the ride effective is that you have no idea what's coming up. You cannot see the drops as they approach. (Playland in Rye, New York, has a coaster called the Dragon Coaster that does much the same thing. This old wooden coaster has a tunnel near the top in the shape of a dragon. Inside, it is dark, and before you are completely out of the tunnel, you are descending the steepest drop.)

THE SPORTS RUSH

Anytime that emotions and great physical sensations go together, there is an opportunity for a high. Sports are a tribute to the link between the body and consciousness.

RUNNING

There are a number of good books on running safely. They outline the proper equipment and techniques. One of the best is *The Complete Book of Running* by James F. Fixx. Nearly anyone can run and get high fairly quickly. Long-distance running releases endorphins into the bloodstream. Endorphins get you high. The problem is that runners get addicted to these endorphins pretty fast. If a week goes by when they are too busy to run, they get quite depressed.

WORKOUTS

Aerobics and workouts work in very much the same way. A good low-impact aerobics class can get you high. Find a qualified teacher and, after checking with your doctor to make sure you are fit enough for an aerobics class, sign up. Each time you experience an endurance threshold, the teacher will tell you to keep going. You shouldn't push through pain but you should challenge your endurance. At each new level there is a slightly different state of consciousness. Usually during the exercise itself you are too concentrated on the activity to focus on your state of consciousness. Next time you work out, rather than going back to work or cooking dinner, take a long walk outside or a quiet sauna. With this kind of high you need to quiet yourself immediately afterward.

During exercise your brain orders extra chemicals, such as adrenaline and endorphins, to support you. When you suddenly stop the exercise, these chemicals remain in your blood. These chemicals are surplus and are not immediately metabolized. The more extra chemicals in your blood, the higher you get. But you need to be receptive and relatively quiet for this to work. Try following an intense workout with a meditation or with one of the other techniques in this book.

COMPETITIVE SPORTS

Most of us have not engaged in competitive sports since high school, and we are missing something. Participation in sports is one of the only times we are allowed to exhibit our animalistic aggressive natures. The mammal within us is invited to surface. This does not mean, however, that you have to get rough. It does mean you have to cut loose.

Winning feels great. If you wrestle someone about your own weight and skill, you will notice a strange thing happen to you. At first you think you are participating in a sport. You have learned certain moves, know the rules, and attempt to pin your opponent. But shortly into the match the combination of your physical effort and your drive to win unleashes an inner strength. From nowhere a will to defeat your opponent emerges. Even if the match has no meaning outside the ring, it feels as though you are involved in a life-or-death struggle. Your primal instincts take over. Hopefully your techniques are automatic. You shouldn't have to think about them. All you need from your consciousness at this point is will and endurance.

When you start to do extremely well in any competitive sport, something even stranger begins to happen. Pro basketball players describe a visual effect that takes place when they are playing their best. They say that everything around them appears to be moving in slow motion. They have all the time in the world to think about what they are going to do. This is more than a rush; it is a moving meditation.

The best sports to try are ones that involve direct interaction with an opponent. Confrontational sports more easily awaken primal energies. Try sports such as hockey, football, basketball, boxing, martial arts, or soccer. They should be endurance sports, which require you to be "on" for sustained periods of time. This way you force your body and mind to acquiesce to your instinctual competitive impulses. You have no choice but to get a rush.

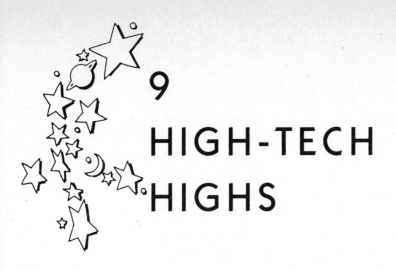

9

HIGH-TECH
HIGHS

For several thousand years the avenue to altered states was ritual and religion. Over the past three decades it has been replaced, at least in the West, by chemicals. The current frontier in brain research, however, is technological. "Brain machines" provide effective, controlled methods of reaching a variety of altered states, by manipulating and "entraining" the brain to reach particular wave patterns. To do this, brain machines utilize sound, light, and/or electromagnetism.

Since the 1920s, scientists have known about the existence of brain waves, and over the following decades they labeled them according to their frequencies: beta, alpha, theta, and delta, in decreasing order. Beta is the brain state of waking awareness. Alpha is a relaxed state and is often used for healing and biofeedback or as a first level for hypnotic induction. Theta is the meditational state. It is profoundly relaxing and is often accompanied by light visual imagery. Delta state is the deepest one we can get to so far. This is the brain wave of deep sleep and out-of-body travel.

Most machines work by creating some kind of phase distortion. For example, a note of a certain frequency is played into one ear and another note slightly out of phase is played into the other. The resulting beat patterns are heard by the brain, which attempts to synchronize itself with that frequency. Add flashing lights at the same or resonant frequencies and the effect is supposedly augmented. The most recent additions to the brain machine arsenal are electromagnetic impulses delivered to the brain by electrodes attached to the head. More specific brain states are also being explored by researchers such as Michael Hutchison, who are attempting to map multiple parameters of the brain states of selected individuals so that their states of consciousness can be re-created in other people.

In all cases the machines promote hemispheric synchronization. Rather than being allowed to work as two separate entities, the left and right halves of the brain are harmonized (in almost exactly the manner that MSH uses in its audiocassettes). The resultant "whole brain thinking" allows for enhanced learning, greater relaxation, behavior modification, better energy, and even periods of euphoria: highs.

Indeed, the most amazing thing about brain machines is that they get you very noticeably altered. They are not subtle like biofeedback machines. Put on a headset and within minutes you will know you are in a different state. If you stay relaxed enough, you should be able to maintain your clarity for several hours after a session. Ideally you will also gain the ability to reach a desired state of consciousness without the machine at all. Still, many people buy these machines for the visuals alone. While most machines actually produce only white or red light, users report seeing a series of multicolored psychedelic images, usually associated with a feeling of euphoria. This is part of the reason why so many brain machines are being bought.

They are fairly expensive. The prices of these units range from a couple of hundred to a couple of thousand dollars, but we am not altogether convinced that the expensive ones perform better anywhere but in the laboratory. Your choice of machine should depend solely on what works for you. No two brains are quite alike. Some people respond more to visuals, others respond to sound or electromagnetic impulses. You need to try before you buy, unless you are wealthy enough make your purchases by trial and error. The best way to sample all of the machines that are available is to attend one of the Whole Life expositions, where nearly everything on the market can be sampled free. If you have time for advanced research, there is an organization run by Michael Hutchison called the Neurotechnologies Research Institute, which gives courses designed to orient you to many of the brain technologies. They can be reached in San Francisco at 415-931-1080, or NRI, 1375 Sutter Street, #402, San Francisco, California 94109. Unless otherwise noted, all the machines mentioned below are available through NRI.

If you decide to purchase a machine of your own, be sure to follow the manufacturer's instructions. If you decide to rent one, do so at a reputable facility, where qualified personnel can instruct you. The best of the brain machines are programmable and flexible. Rather than having just a few settings, they let you program an entire session. This way you can decide, for example, just how long you would like to be in alpha state before you move on to theta, and so on. You also gain control of which parameters you wish to change and how gradually they should move. The cheapest units are not programmable, but just like cheap, nonprogrammable CD players, they provide just about the same quality of experience.

The most expensive of the popular units is called DAVID (Digital Audio Visual Integration Device). It is a professional sound-and-light machine, with probably the highest quality goggles (they're lined with special incandescent bulbs). There are synthesized sound effects in the machine's memory, as well as inputs for tapes or a microphone for a therapist. It is even equipped with some rudimentary biofeedback devices, so it can play back in the rhythm of your own heartbeat.

The DAVID Jr. costs about $900 to $1,000 and is portable. While it is not as flexible as the DAVID machine, it does provide the same types of sounds, and similar features. Its visuals are on a less-expensive electroluminescent panel.

The David Jr. unit also has something called the Ganzfeld feature: a blank viewing field in the color of your choice. The Ganzfeld effect is in some ways a more profound deprivation than darkness. By stimulating the brain with a constant, unchanging visual field, you can attain the "blank-out" effect, where you lose touch altogether with the visual apparatus. This is not seeing blackness, but rather not seeing at all. There is a machine called the Theta One (which costs only $150 to $200) that features just a Ganzfeld effect and a brain-synchronization tape.

The most programmable of the machines around so

far is called Mindseye, an audiovisual synthesizer capable of playing back up to three hours of programming. At about $800, we would recommend it only for veteran mind-machine operators. It is quite complex and designed more for programmers than for users. If you are interested in advanced brain research, you probably already know about this machine. Otherwise begin with a simpler model.

One of the easiest ways to get started is with a unit called Inner Quest, a relatively inexpensive ($500) yet flexible machine. It also works with sound, light, and a built-in Sony Walkman cassette player. Similar to the Inner Quest is a unit called the MC2, available for about $350 through Light and Sound Research, 6991 East Camelback Road, Suite C-151, Scottsdale, Arizona 85251 (602-941-4459). It boasts the same features for less money. Most other light-and-sound machines fall into this general category. Again, try them for yourself.

The other main category of brain machines incorporates a pulsed electromagnetic stimulation of the brain. It sounds dangerous, but so far it's still legal (although one of the machines requires a prescription). Hutchinson backs a unit called Alpha Pacer II, for about $500, which uses sound and light in addition to cranial electrostimulation. Robert Anton Wilson, in his review of these products (*Magical Blend*, July 1989) highly endorses the Endo-Max machine, which costs about $200 to $250 and is extremely portable. It uses only electro-stimulation and audio. Both of these units have been used to treat chemical dependency and seem to work something like modern acupuncture: An electrode is attached to an acupuncture point, then a charge is passed through the point to another one. The sensation is a light tapping. We did not experience a high during our sessions on these kinds of machines, but we did have a feeling of greater energy and well-being for many hours afterward.

Hutchison's center also provides access to a machine called Lumatron, which works by photic stimulation. (If purchased privately, the machine would cost $7,900; but it includes a four-day seminar.) Invented by Dr. John Downing, the machine works by stimulating the brain with short bursts of light at varying but particular wavelengths. It is supposed to help regulate the hypothalamic-discharge rate, and eventually balance the neuroendocrine system.

As far as we are concerned, audiocassettes like those offered by MSH work about as well as any of these machines—at least as far as getting you to a particular brain state. Admittedly, using a live, programmable, computer source allows you to custom-design an entire session and even choose your target brain frequency to the nearest hundredth of a hertz; but not everyone needs or wants that kind of control or that kind of expense. Along with Brother Charles, the best tapes around right now for all-around brainplay are the Psycho-Immunology tapes by Acoustic Brain Research (P.O. Box 3214, Chapel Hill, North Carolina 27515).

10
THRILL OF THE
OUTDOORS

Natural highs are some of the easiest ones to come by. Unfortunately we usually associate natural scenery with nightmarish family trips or boring state-park excursions. If we can rid ourselves of our conclusions about what nature has to offer consciousness, we will be free to interact with the elements that created consciousness in the first place. In nature, more than anywhere else, it is possible for us to experience how we are linked both physically and spiritually to everything else. The euphoria associated with this realization is a natural high.

Your level of interaction with nature depends on you.

You can drive for an hour in your car and look out over a vista or you can fly to the Himalayas for a two-month camping trip. The depth of your experience of the sublime does not depend on how long or how intensely you are prepared to rough it. Rather it depends on your sensitivity to your environment and the flexibility of your state of mind. It took our friend, Nancy, three full days staring at rocks in the middle of Utah before she could let go of her Los Angeles reality. Ever since, all she needs is a good half hour of uninterrupted time in nature to get to the same state of consciousness.

Why we get high in nature is unimportant here. It probably has something to do with the fact that for tens of thousands of years human beings lived in natural settings. We do have a natural habitat. Returning to nature gives us a sense of well-being because it resonates with something deep inside us. We know that the ego and mind depend on the illusion of individuality for their survival. It is quite easy to see yourself as separate from everything else when your environment is made of inorganic materials and man-made surfaces. When you are in nature, however, you become one with your surroundings. Surfaces are porous and interactive. And while the boundary between what you call *self* and what you call *other* gets hazy, your experience of life begins to get much clearer. Your senses improve as they delight in their interaction with their environment. (Smelling, for example, is easier when the air is sweet.) Rather than resisting life and getting in your own way, you begin to enjoy each moment of aliveness. You approach bliss. John Denver was right.

TRAVEL

Most of us already know something about travel. The trick to traveling for the sake of consciousness is to do it for that purpose alone. Do not go sightseeing, souvenir buying, or relative visiting. Do not try to make time. Let go of "civilized" reality and immerse yourself as fully as you can in nature. There are a number of good travel agents and wilderness groups catering to people who seek spiritual travel experiences. Many are advertised in New Age magazines. The following are some to try:

Above the Clouds Trekking, P.O. Box 398, Worcester, Massachusetts 01602 (800-233-4499). International tours.

The Great Round Vision Quests, P.O. Box 201, Bodega, California 94922 (707-874-2736). U.S. trips.

Mountain Travel, 1398 Solano Avenue, Albany, California 94706 (415-527-8100). Domestic and international.

Odyssey Tours, 1821 Wilshire Boulevard, Santa Monica, California 90403 (213-453-1042). Asia.

Off the Beaten Path, 109 East Main Street, Bozeman, Montana 59715 (406-586-1311). Rocky Mountains.

Power Places Tours, 28802 Alta Laguna Boulevard, Laguna Beach, California 92651 (714-497-5138). Domestic and international.

If you have no money to travel, there are groups (other than the Peace Corps) that allow you to volunteer some services in exchange for camping or travel expenses. The best is the American Hiking Society (703-385-3253), in Washington, D.C. They can even let you know about opportunities for fire watching, where you live alone in the middle of a state park in a house up on stilts. Your job is to stare out and watch for forest fires.

We still think the best way to get altered by traveling is to do it by yourself, or with a chosen partner, and to have as unplanned an itinerary as possible. The trip should feel as open-ended as possible. The easiest thing to do is take a couple of weeks off from work, get a tent and some sleeping bags, hop in the car, and drive. Just go. Take a map if you want. You don't have to camp out. You can stay in motels, or sleep in the car (where it's still legal). Take long walks on nature trials. Lose track of the time of day and the day of the week. Trips are easygoing, relatively risk-free excursions. We get the most high when we are relaxed and open. There are also other ways to get high outside.

SURVIVAL HIGHS

There is a high to feeling keenly aware of your own ability to survive. There are many wilderness courses (some are available through the above groups) that teach you how to survive in nature. There is a lot to be said for this kind of experience. First, most of us believe we are incapable of learning how to live off the land. Gaining an ability as tangible as this directly contradicts our self-images of unworthiness and ineptitude. This is why so many drug-rehabilitation and behavior-modification groups include outdoor wilderness trips in their programs.

The more completely you interact with nature, the greater your experience of oneness with it. The ability to survive in nature depends on your ability to live harmoniously with it. Western civilization paves over nature in order to grow. Real survival skills have nothing to do with taming nature. They allow you to perceive the way nature is moving and to stay alive by positioning yourself properly within that movement. You become part of the organization of the woods around you.

BEFRIENDING THE ELEMENTS

There is a beautiful book called *The Findhorn Garden* that tells the true story of how a group of people used the advice of devas to create a farm on essentially infertile soil. Their experience demonstrates the necessity of cooperating with nature and opening the intelligences that can help us gain awareness: "We have not only to cooperate with the nature kingdoms, but we have to allow them to become one with us. Through this marriage, we are more truly human." If, after reading *The Findhorn Garden,* you want to get involved in this particular path, you can contact Peter Caddy, who is one of founders of the Findhorn community, through Wilson and Lake International, 1 Appian Way, #704-8, South San Francisco, California 94080 (415-589-0352). He conducts tours of Findhorn and arranges for people to join the Findhorn community for various lengths of time.

Of course you can always begin on your own. There are many books available on organic gardening, so you do not have to reinvent the wheel. Luckily there are even plans for creating a garden large enough to feed yourself with an area only as big as a large terrace or section of rooftop, so don't worry about the fact that you live in an apartment.

CULTURE AS NATURE

Traveling to a place that is completely foreign to you, even if it is completely civilized, can get you into some very new head spaces. The technique we are describing here is a sort of familiarity deprivation. All you do is travel to a place where you do not speak the language or understand any of the customs. Amazing things begin to happen to you.

Your view of humanity changes. There are many things you associate with personhood that are not necessarily linked with being human. These are aspects of social behavior that your society might take for granted but another might ignore completely. To feel the effect of this contrast, you must resist all forms of English-speaking media, and familiar settings. There is no point in going to Jakarta and then watching U.S. TV and eating in McDonald's. (Although there is a strange kind of high to be derived from something like that as well.)

For most of us an extended trip abroad is necessary for the kind of radical mind shift we seek. The best places to try are usually in the Far East, Indonesia, or Africa, although some New Yorkers experience this kind of culture shock simply by traveling to Los Angeles for a weekend.

11

FROM THE
OUTSIDE IN

There is a large physical component to getting high. In fact many of us only know that we are high when we feel physically different. It is as if our sensory functions need to be altered in order to confirm that we are experiencing a real change. While it is true that changes in mind and spirit can have external repercussions, the physical body, when manipulated willfully, can also alter the experience of the consciousness it houses. Getting high is a two-way street.

There are many physical therapies that act on the mind through the body. The neural pathways connecting muscle and skin to the brain provide a therapist access to your consciousness. Thus a good massage can put your brain into alpha or delta state. A qualified doctor of acupuncture can alter the flow of life energy, *chi,* in your body, changing your experience of life itself. Similarly you can alter your perceptions of reality by altering your body's sensations.

In this chapter we'll briefly outline the theory and practice of a few of the physical therapies that alter consciousness, then describe things you can do to yourself. Of course anything like acupuncture, rolfing, or therapeutic massage must only be performed by licensed, qualified persons.

ACUPUNCTURE AND ACUPRESSURE

These are two of the main branches of Oriental medicine. Just as many of the greatest mind-altering substances came out of Western pharmacological research, the several-thousand-year-old history of Oriental medicine is not without its own nooks and crannies. Oriental medicine works by regulating *chi* in the body. Unlike allopathic (most Western) medicine, which battles enemy diseases to restore health, Eastern doctors see illness as an imbalance of energy. The systems of acupuncture and acupressure restore the *chi* to its proper level and circulation. Not being high can be seen as an imbalance. Either your energy level is high but misdirected and blocked, or your energy is just not high enough in the first place.

Both of these conditions can be alleviated through the practice of Oriental medicine. To locate blocks, the practitioner takes something similar to pulses from the main meridian lines of the body. One meridian is associated with the liver, another with the heart, and so on. A practitioner can tell by feeling the pulse that a meridian is blocked somewhere. To eliminate the blockages of the flow of *chi,* the doctor stimulates the meridian at a specific point with a needle or the fingers, sending energy to the point of blockage until it is cleared. If there is simply not enough energy in a particular meridian, the doctor may perform something called moxibustion, in which an herbal moxi stick is burned directly over an acupuncture point. The heat generated by the moxi stick energizes the weak meridian.

To get high from acupuncture or acupressure requires that you not be sick when you visit the practitioner. You must go when you already feel pretty good. When the doctor asks why you have come, tell him you want more energy, or want to learn to relax better, depending upon your current state. You could also simply explain that you

are visiting him for your general well-being and a balancing of your *chi* energies. The doctor will take pulses from
different points on your wrist, determine the energy flow
in each of your meridians, and then bring you into a
treatment room. You will lie on a table and the doctor will
either use needles or finger pressure to stimulate certain
points along the meridians that need balancing.

Getting high off this can be felt as a subtle change or
as an obvious one, depending on how aggressively the
therapist chooses to work. In any case ask what is being
done to you so that you can try to visualize the effects. If
you are told that a certain acupuncture point in your foot
relates to your liver, for example, try to imagine the
meridian along which the *chi* is supposed to be traveling.
The high of acupuncture and acupressure is a result of the
rebalancing of the *chi* in your body. While intensely
relaxing, the experience is also mind altering. You feel as
though your whole body were being adjusted to a single
frequency. Instead of having many disconnected parts, all
doing their own thing, your mind, body, and spirit
become relaxed and united.

This state of being is much more energetic than it
seems. As one learns in the *chi*-related martial arts, the best
defense is to stay completely receptive. Similarly the state
of highest potential energy is a very relaxed one. When the
session is over, do not run outside, eat a big lunch, and get

caught in traffic. Don't smoke a cigarette or drink a cup of coffee. Just relax, maybe walk around outside and look at nature. You will find that you see the world differently. You may even feel disoriented. The potential difference (voltage) between different parts of your organism has been evened out. Places your energy has been unnecessarily held are now open. Most importantly the connection between your brain/consciousness and your energy fields has been redefined. You are now free to experience life free of many of the barriers you were holding on to unconsciously. You may feel more relaxed, but you are actually much more alive.

MASSAGE

Hopefully you have already experienced a good massage at some point in your life. If you have not, you are missing something extraordinary. In finding a masseur or masseuse, look for someone with some New Age experience. We would be the last to advocate the New Age marketing blitz, but this is usually the best channel to find people who do bodywork related to consciousness expansion. If possible, meet your prospective bodyworker ahead of time. Use your intuition. If you like the person, great. If you feel at all funny about him or her, find another. This person will be in intimate contact with you. If you think the person is a creep, you won't benefit a drop.

A massage is a wonderful way of telling yourself you deserve pleasure. Most of us feel so unworthy that we deny ourselves pleasure for pleasure's sake. We have sex because we are "in a relationship." We go to therapists because it is "healthy." Get a massage because it feels great. Don't worry about anything. Accept the gift of another human being's hands. Treat yourself. A massage is time for you to relax and for someone else to work. Realizing this is half the high.

Depending upon you and the particular massage you get, you can move into any number of states of consciousness. We have gone into alpha and delta states. We have friends who have even gone out-of-body during massages. Do not worry about what you are experiencing. Just relax. Many people are afraid of getting sexually aroused during a massage. Give in to whatever feeling arises and it will probably pass. Suppressing it will only make it worse. Worse case: The masseuse sees you have an erection or hears you moan. Big deal. She has seen it all before. You may want to laugh, cry, or scream. Cut loose. You will be told if you do something wrong.

The beginning of a massage is the only difficult part. You will feel where you are holding both physically and emotionally. But once you begin to let go, everything will let go. Your only job is to lie there and relax. Usually what happens after the initial letting-go phase is like sleep, only deeper. You may worry that you are no longer conscious of what the masseuse is doing and that you are missing something. This is ridiculous and will soon pass. Let the masseuse worry about your body, and let your mind float free. Massage gets you high because your body is in someone else's hands. You are being cared for. You are safe.

After a massage follow the same rules as for acupuncture. The state of consciousness is different. You will probably feel more loving, huggy, and want to be around people rather than alone in nature. Try taking a warm shower or whirlpool, or just take a nice nap. It's a great idea to precede the massage with a sauna or hot tub.

ROLFING

Rolfing is a form of massage based on a technique developed by Ida Rolf in the 1950s. Rolf's methods of massage seek to rebalance the muscle and tissue throughout the body by direct manipulation. The muscles have become unbalanced because of the shocks, injuries, and upsets we have experienced throughout our lives. For example, if you were hit for doing something wrong when you were a child, you might still be carrying the stress of that event in the memory of your muscle. As a result you are still holding on to that memory in your mind and body.

A good Rolfer relaxes your surface muscles enough to manipulate the deepest ones in your body. The Rolfer seeks to break up calcium deposits and restretch muscles to their natural state. This takes ten one-hour sessions and is supposed to be permanent. Be careful picking your Rolfer. Certification and a good recommendation are musts. This is a very deep form of bodywork, and there are many people out there claiming to be Rolfers who are not.

Rolfing gets you high for a pretty obvious reason. In addition to being a form of massage, Rolfing relieves you of physical and emotional hang-ups. If you can let go of an injury, guilt, pain, or grudge that has taken hold in your body for years, imagine how much lighter you will feel. Your entire relationship to gravity changes as you enter into life with a clean slate. During the session you may relive the event that led to your stress in the first place, and this may not be pleasurable. But getting truly and fully high is not always a pleasurable process. The results are what we are after.

Ida Rolf is an inspired woman. She understands the relationship of the mind to the body, and of both to the rest of reality. Her way of thinking is accessible to us in *Ida*

Rolf Talks About Rolfing and Physical Reality, by Rosemary Feitis. Unfortunately many people who practice Rolfing are not as inspired as Rolf herself. They seem to think of their work as an invasive retraining of the body rather than simply allowing the body to move into the place it really wants to be anyway. To find a good Rolfer, we recommend contacting the Rolf Institute directly, at Box 1868, Boulder, Colorado 80306.

SPAS AND HOT SPRINGS

If you are serious about getting to the mind through the body, you should treat yourself to several days at a good spa. New spas are opening all the time and provide a pretty cheap but totally consuming vacation experience. They range from about $500 to $2,000 per week for full use of the facilities. (You can find spas for more if you look hard enough, but chances are their facilities are no better—only the decor.) Special treatments and therapies are usually extra. The best sourcebook for finding a good spa is Ed and Judy Colbert's *The Spa Guide.* They list the best spas and health resorts in North America and the Caribbean. They even list cruise ships that offer spa facilities. The best recommendation the Colberts make is that you prepare for your spa visit by eating and living a little more healthily before you get to the spa. This way you will not have to go through any withdrawal while you are on vacation.

The best spas to try are those that are built at natural hot springs and hot pools. Water heated geothermically is rich with minerals that are good for you; they tend to help the water work on you more effectively. Most natural spas also boast a large variety of therapies that healthy people can use to expand their consciousness. These include herbal wraps, hydro (water) therapies of all kinds, thalasso therapy (seawater therapy), mud baths, all kinds of massage, yoga, and exercise. Spas are a "back to nature" trip, but a luxurious way to do it. Always feel free to take part in only as much as you want. Many spas have a regimented atmosphere. They are for unhealthy, overweight people who want to be told what to do. Try, instead, to find a spa that lets you choose how little or how much you wish to take part.

As with any physical inroad to the psyche, you are the boss. It is your body. The key is to relax and let your body serve you the way it was meant to.

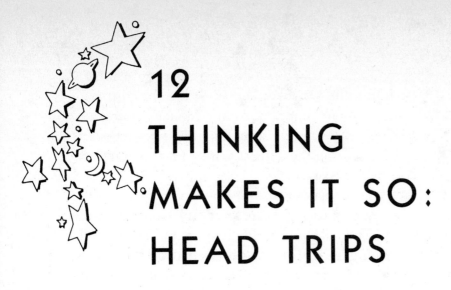

12

THINKING
MAKES IT SO:
HEAD TRIPS

While scoffed at by nature lovers, body people, and even some gurus, the path of the intellect can be a very rewarding mind-altering experience. In addition, it usually leaves you feeling smarter, or at least having something to talk about. The great intellects of all ages invariably circulated among contemporary writers, artists, occultists, and bohemians. What they all had in common was that they got off on what they did.

The reason the intellect can get you high is that it brings you closer to understanding higher truths. Contemplating the possibility of time travel, for example, forces the thinker to grapple with the notion of time itself. Pondering Jung's theory of the collective unconscious can lead to insights about thought, the interconnectedness of all living things, or even reincarnation. The intellect is an avenue to experiencing the highest principles and grandest movements of the cosmos.

In fact contemplating *anything* will eventually lead you to larger questions. One can contemplate computers, for example. The machines "think" in a binary, digital code. Everything is 1/0 or yes/no. Is that the way the whole universe is? The yin/yang? Is that what they meant? You see our point. What allows the great contemplators to think through to states of altered consciousness is their ability to ramble mentally, unedited and unashamed, through the deepest regions of their minds.

The joy of contemplation usually comes from seeing how a tidbit can be generalized to explain something huge. The players of Herman Hesse's Glass Bead Game (in *Magister Ludi*) had a new, universal language that allowed them to ponder any branch of thought and relate it empirically to any other. They would develop a theme from the rules of one system and understand how it applied to another. The famous mathematician Paul Erdos believes mathematics is not an abstract but an existing world that the human mind actively explores. When someone comes up with a powerful new property or formula, such as Einstein's $E = mc^2$, Erdos exclaims, "That's in the book." What he means is that there are only a few organizing principles in the world. Through a specific inquiry, one can reach conclusions of epic proportions. But even more importantly in light of our own book's purpose, the intellect can bring your consciousness to unexplored regions.

There is a famous story in Richard Ellman's biography of James Joyce. The great author brought his mentally ill daughter, Lucia, to her twentieth psychiatrist, Carl Jung. After examining her, Jung sorrowfully informed Joyce that Lucia was suffering from a serious schizoid disorder. But Joyce protested that his daughter's ramblings also made profound sense: much of what she said, heard, and saw were the same images that Joyce contemplated and wrote about. Jung explained that both father and daughter were at the bottom of the same river, but that while Lucia was sinking, Joyce was diving.

We bring this story up not to frighten but to inspire. The intellect does provide access to the hidden regions— the places you go to during a mystical experience. The intellect serves as fuel for a number of different vehicles that can get you high. Try any of these, or just sit with a good, smart friend and start talking.

THE TRADITION OF PARADOX

"What is the sound of one hand clapping?" calls to mind the blind old monk on the TV show *Kung Fu* who puzzled little Grasshopper for ten years with this kind of question. Most religious orders have volumes of literature devoted to explanations of and answers to riddles their great masters and teachers left for them. Monks often spend their days pondering a single word choice by Buddha, Krishna, or Jesus.

Often, however, these questions were never meant to be answered. It was by studying the riddle and moving your mind in the shapes and contortions a particular riddle produces that you were to find enlightenment. In this same manner we can reexamine the Zen koans, Sufi paradoxes, and Kabbalistic puzzles in order to reach higher states of consciousness through the intellect.

ZEN KOANS

Zen koans are philosophical riddles designed to illuminate. They are supposed to be unsolvable without an alteration in consciousness. To understand the question, you must move out of normal consciousness. The insight associated with solving the koan is not intellectual, but rather comes from outside the cerebral dimension. You ponder a koan such as "What was your face before you were born?" Whatever you are doing, you ponder this question. It is the mantra of your meditations, meals, and work. The koan is unsolvable through logic. The frustration becomes unbearable, until eventually your mind moves into another dimension in order solve it.

With this illumination comes a lightness of being as you understand the applications of the koan to other aspects of life. We haven't pursued intellectual paths as structured as koans but can recommend *The Zen Koan* by Isshu Miura and Ruth Fuller Sasaki as an excellent source of these kinds of puzzles. Another great starting place is *Zen Flesh, Zen Bones* by Paul Reps.

If you'd like to try working on a koan, here's a sample: The monk asks, "What is Buddha?" His master responds, "This mind is not Buddha." According to Master Mu-mon, anyone who fully understands this exchange is a master of Zen. Another: A master holds up his cane and poses the riddle "If you say this cane is short, you are negating its reality. If you don't say it is short, you are ignoring the fact. What will you say?"

SUFI TEACHING STORIES

In a tradition similar to the Zen masters, the Sufis also engage in long contemplations of paradox, hoping, too, that the working out of these problems will lead to higher consciousness. Instead of posing riddles, the Sufis generally tell stories for which enlightenment is a prerequisite to understanding. These teaching stories, or dervish tales, all end in apparent non sequitur. Finding the connection—making sense of the characters' actions or words—releases the spiritual energy that thrusts one farther on the path to enlightenment.

Idries Shah is a leader of the Sufi tradition and has written several volumes of teaching stories. According to Shah, these stories have inner dimensions that teach more and more as the student develops. One good example is a story called "The Cradle," in which a man, whose wife has given birth to a baby boy, goes to a carpenter and orders a cradle. The carpenter tells the man to come back in a week. The man returns, week after week, but the cradle is not finished. Eventually the child grows up and has a son of his own. The father suggests that his son approach the carpenter for the cradle that was ordered so many years ago. When the son goes to the carpenter, he is chided, "I will not be rushed in my work by your family's obsession with you want!"

Still, Sufi masters warn against using these stories, or any practices for that matter, in order to produce highs. Although the Sufi stories do possess the ability to transmit altered states of consciousness, the states themselves are not to be seen as goals, or they will do more damage than good. To the Sufis, this is equivalent to a jackal scavenging the leftovers of a lion.

In Sufism, as with almost any of the religious paths suggested in this chapter, the seeker must be ready to commit more than a passing fancy to the philosophies and practices. These are not highs that can be easily experienced in one afternoon's effort. The following practice is no exception.

KABBALAH

Kabbalah is said to have developed out of spiritual necessity. The Jews of this tradition believe that there was once a kind of cosmic harmony on earth, perpetuated by the proper placement of the original Ten Commandments in an ark in the first Temple. It is said to have functioned like a crystal in a great cosmic radio. At this time in history prophets walked the earth and knew that invasion was imminent and that the Temple would be destroyed. The Jews constructed an elaborate subterranean labyrinth for the ark of the covenant. Meanwhile the prophets, knowing their time on earth was limited, created Scriptures, which, properly deciphered, hold the secrets of the universe and the keys to restoring harmony on the planet.

These works include the Torah and some of the later books of the Old Testament.

For reasons they did not even fully understand, the Jews passed on these Scriptures, following strict rules for exactly how they were to be transcribed and pronounced. Early Jewish scholars began slowly to decipher these texts, using techniques ranging from numerology to elaborate diagrams of the order of the universe. For the dedicated intellectual it's supposed to be pretty rewarding stuff. These early mystics used the Psalms as a starting place to visualize God and heaven but eventually learned techniques to move past such concrete images and experience the pure divine light at the throne of God. Unfortunately Kabbalah just isn't the kind of path you can try out on a free afternoon. We don't have the space to demonstrate the kinds of enlightenment potentiated by these studies, but we assure you that for Westerners especially they are quite rewarding. It's likely that part of the thrill of Kabbalah for us is the fact that the main source of mystical energy is the Bible, which has been right under our noses (sometimes pushed there) since we were kids. The most obviously mystical sections are the first chapter of Genesis and the first chapter of Ezekiel (the most magical of the prophets). The other main source of inspiration for the mystics is contemplation of the Cosmic Tree (the Tree of Life), an elaborate diagram of the structure of the universe, as well as the levels of consciousness. For further study, first try *Kabbalah: Tradition of Hidden Knowledge*, by Z'ev ben Shimon Halevi. It's easy to read, well diagrammed, and written by a fine teacher of Jewish mysticism. Also excellent are *The Way of Kabbalah*, by the same author, and *Path of the Kabbalah*, by David Shienkin.

BETTING SYSTEMS

Being able to predict the future has its obvious benefits. But the ancient systems of astrology, Tarot, the I Ching, and the Runes did not develop merely as divinatory tools; they attempt to explain the nature of time and our motion through it. Studying any of these systems can lead to great spiritual insight, whether or not you care to know how wealthy your next lover will be.

All of these techniques identify trends and cycles in the universe. The earth seems to circle the sun every 365¼ days. Certain things seem to happen in certain months. The positions of the planets seem to influence or at least indicate forces at work on earth. Time seems cyclical rather than linear. These ideas are based on a holographic view of the world: the tea leaves in the bottom of your cup are part of the motion of the universe and can thus reflect the movement of all of nature, assuming the reader has a proper method of divination. Similarly six tosses of three I Ching coins produce one of sixty-four hexagrams that indicates the tosser's state of being or answers his or her questions.

Our interest here is not necessarily in practicing these techniques but in exploring how they were developed and how they work. If intellectual highs are derived by momentarily understanding our connection to everything else around us, then surely the study of forms that demonstrate this fact is in order.

The best initial sources for this kind of study are:

Astrology:

The Inner Sky by Steven Forrest

The Art and Practice of Chinese Astrology by Derek Walters

Tarot:

The Mystic Tarot (comes with a deck of cards) by Juliet Sharman-Burke and Liz Greene

Motherpeace: A Way to the Goddess through Myth, Art, and Tarot by Vicki Noble

A New Handbook for the Apprentice by Eileen Connolly

I Ching:

The Taoist I Ching trans. by Thomas Cleary

The Philosophy of the I Ching by Carol K. Anthony

Runes:

The Book of Runes by Ralph Blum

NOT FOR NERDS ONLY: SCIENCE AND MATH

Descriptive math and science—the kind most of us learned in school—are pretty boring. The reason we were taught these subjects with a practical orientation is obvious: What sells science to Western society is the fact that it's useful. Math can be used to calculate deficits and interest rates, while science is applied to determine how much gas a certain engine needs to go four hundred miles or how many calories are in a bowl of tapioca pudding. These are not useless facts; but the experiments or calculations involved in obtaining them rarely get you high. The transcendental quality of math and science—which is what interests us here—is that they attempt to make sense out of chaos. The manner in which they do so differs, however.

MATH AS NIRVANA

Math assumes perfection. It has its own reality and exists independently of the natural world. A certain equation will always lead to a certain graph. Newton's equations for harmonic motion (a pendulum or spring) would remain perfect on their own terms, even if something in the real world were to change. Math is correct. Eventually the real world, as seemingly chaotic as it is, will be reduced to a system of equations. Finding the equations that explain the cosmos leads to an expansion of consciousness.

Learning math is like studying history. It is generally taught in the order it was discovered. We learn arithmetic, algebra, geometry, then trigonometry (the combination of algebra and geometry), and from trigonometry we deduce calculus. There is beauty just in learning these subjects. Assuming you aren't worried about a grade, or memorizing a theorem or identity, there is joy to be derived from finding an elegant solution to a seemingly complex equation. Most of us hated math in school because the focus was on being able to solve problems with memorized techniques in a short amount of time. If you don't have to memorize what you're reading, you can follow the arguments and observe the workings of the mathematical systems in the same way you might explore the workings of an intricate Swiss watch.

Math gets really fun, however, when it is in the hands of people like Ralph Abraham. This University of California at Santa Cruz math professor took a day off in 1967 to explore his consciousness. When he returned seven years later, he had traveled all over Europe and Asia, spent months in caves, and experienced the Logos. Sitting in the dark in the mountain caves of Tibet, Abraham had striking visions of vibratory fields. Only later did he realize that these visions could be considered three-dimensional graphs of dynamic systems. Somehow nirvana and math were related. Abraham is spending most of his time communicating his findings to the likes of us. He has written four picture books about the geometry of behavior, which read more like children's books than math texts, so don't be intimidated. While he knows that his experience of the dynamics of behavior is probably incommunicable, he does hope that "perhaps a visual representation would excite the full field in the viewer's mind through morphic resonance." That is, because the pictures in the book are visual representations of a deep reality, they excite a recognition response in those who view and understand them. For us, this has worked, and we highly recommend Abraham's series of books: *Dynamics: The Geometry of Behavior*, by Ralph Abraham and C. D. Shaw. There are currently four volumes: *Periodic Behavior, Chaotic Behavior, Global Behavior,* and *Bifurcation Behavior.* Ariel Press also boasts a catalog of other math texts and publications on the cutting edge of consciousness exploration.

GETTING OFF ON THE SCIENTIFIC MODEL

Unlike math, science knows that it is probably wrong about most everything. We've all had a science teacher in high school tell us smugly that half of what we were to learn that year would probably prove to be wrong. The beauty of science is the evolution of the scientific model. This model—huge, clunky, and riddled with "exceptions"—attempts to explain reality. It got its start when people wanted to know what stars were, or why fire worked, and was developed by Descartes and Galileo, through Newton, to Einstein, and now to us. So if at one time atoms were believed to be the fundamental particle, it was just a matter of time before a scientist realized this could not be true, hypothesized what a subatomic particle might look like, then experimented further to test his hypothesis. Even if he was "proved" correct, it was only a matter of time before someone else realized that there was yet a smaller fundamental particle. After that the scientific model made an even more radical change as scientists wondered if matter really exists at all or if the fundamental particle is really just a form of energy. You get the general idea here.

At one time the scientific model assumed that Newton's laws worked for everything. All reality was explainable by the laws that govern the movement of masses on earth. Then we realized this was not the case and have been trying to explain it ever since. Quantum physics, in a desperate attempt to save what was left of the model, proposed that Newton's laws work on earth for things of average size but that other laws would be needed in order to explain subatomic particles and the movement of planets. It's been a free-for-all ever since, which is why it's so interesting.

The current movement in science could even be considered spiritual. Scientists have become aware of the interconnectedness of all things. In theory, at least, positrons from the same nucleus will maintain their identical direction of spin, even if separated over huge distances. If the spin of one of these positrons were changed, the other one would change, too, even though it is in no physical proximity. Similarly when attempting to create new crytalline structures, scientists may work weeks or months trying to get the atoms to structure themselves in a certain way. Once they do, however, and a new crystal is created, the same crystal structure will appear spontaneously in labs throughout the world. It is as if once the atoms are taught to align in a certain way, all atoms of the same type somehow gain this ability as well. In a strange echo of Jung's theory of the collective unconscious, the behavior of these particles is likened to a behavior of animals called morphogenetic resonance. At Harvard William McDougal taught a large population of rats how to go through a certain maze. Spontaneously and unexplainably rats in Europe gained this knowledge too.

Places to begin this kind of exploration are *Beyond the Quantum,* by Michael Talbot; *A Brief History of Time,* by Stephen Hawking; and *The Tao of Physics,* by Fritjof Capra. Or go to your local university bookstore and browse the shelves, or audit courses that sound interesting. Many colleges offer courses with titles like "Physics for Poets" or "Philosophy of Science," usually taught by scientists with a need to share their highs.

MYTHOLOGY AND PHILOSOPHY

Much more popular with intellectual seekers these days are the paths of the seemingly less scientific thinkers. Men like Joseph Campbell share a sense of the "oneness" of all consciousness through their exhaustive research of nearly all the world's mythologies. In *The Power of Myth* Campbell even shares his concept of bliss and his belief that all people can find it for themselves. Rather than search these kinds of books for explicit answers, though, one should get high through the experience of understanding what the authors are communicating.

People like Campbell, Timothy Leary, Alan Watts, or Aldous Huxley are all trying to communicate an experience outside of language. Poets of the intellect, these men have created works of literature that transcend language, and they create the experience of oneness that is being high. Through the intellectual understanding of our place as part, center, and full manifestation of the universe, we reach a state of bliss.

Campbell's work has been quite popular ever since the series of interviews he did with Bill Moyers aired on PBS. These interviews are available on videotape at your local video store, and we recommend them as an introduction to Campbell's body of work. *The Power of Myth* is a compilation of these interviews, and reading it can be an experience of bliss. An advocate of reaching and attaining bliss, Campbell explains how by following your rapture and your bliss, you may successfully bring your consciousness into true being.

The list of brilliant thinkers goes on and on. Of particular interest might be the works of Carl G. Jung, a psychologist who spent his life developing the theory of the collective unconscious and exploring the archetypal images shared by all people of all times. Start out with a collection of essays so that you can decide which branch of his voluminous text most interests you.

Alan Watts was probably this century's last great pure philosopher. His works are available in print or on cassette from Alan Watts Electronic Educational Programs, Box 938, Point Reyes Station, California 94956 (415-663-9102). A good departure point into his mind would be his autobiography, *In My Own Way* (New York: Vintage Books, 1973), which chronicles the development of his thinking. Watts was a student of Zen who got "turned on" to psychedelics in the sixties, then became a popular philosopher with the intellectual wing of the Beat generation. His description of an LSD trip in *The Joyous Cosmology* surpasses even Huxley's *Doors of Perception*. In one particularly vivid passage, Watts describes how he realized that the passive and the active are parts of the same energy. He had caught a floating dandelion seed in his fingers and held it by one hair. He watched it wiggle as if it were struggling to get away, and then Watts realized that although the movement was caused by the wind—and thus not "intentional"—the action was dictated by the seed having enough "intelligence" to possess winglike hairs that could fly on the wind. In this way the seed's passive role could be considered active.

Also of interest are Terence and Dennis McKenna, who originally used psychedelics to develop a theory of time and consciousness. Their most interesting book, *The Invisible Landscape: Mind, Hallucinogens, and the I Ching* is out of print, but can probably be found in the psychology libraries of most universities. The McKennas are very unorthodox thinkers, but they support all of their notions with exhaustive scientific research. While a little dense for some readers, this work is a mind-expanding argument for the oneness and circularity of our existence. Terence and Dennis compare the collective consciousness to a giant hologram. A hologram is a three-dimensional picture. The interesting thing about a hologram is that, when broken, each piece can produce the entire image, but in less detail. The McKennas believe that, like the hologram, the collective consciousness is the sum of many contiguous fragments—our individual minds. Each of our minds contains the essence of reality, but in less detail than all the pieces can render it collectively. The nature of reality can only be ultimately resolved when the individual pieces can join together.

Easier access to the McKenna minds is in a "talking book" (audio cassettes) called *True Hallucinations,* available through Sound Photosynthesis, P.O. Box 2111, Mill Valley, California 94942. They also carry the audio works of philosophers including Robert Anton Wilson, Timothy Leary, John Lilly, and William Burroughs.

Easier to understand but still somewhat transcendental are books by Joseph Chilton Pearce. *The Crack in the Cosmic Egg* is a good first step in the exploration of philosophy as an intellectual path toward bliss.

This seems like the best place to mention one of our favorite philosophical books. It's a fairly optimistic and very convincing argument for the imminent radical evolution of the human species to a higher form of consciousness. *Unknown Man* by Yatri is a beautifully illustrated volume that encompasses everything from schizophrenia to Buddhafield while maintaining the tone of a good after-dinner discussion. Reading the book and accepting the fact that someday soon we may all be high, all the time, is mind-altering in itself.

READ ANY GOOD BOOKS LATELY?

Lastly, fiction provides immediate access to the thought processes of transcendental thinkers. The rule of thumb is to find authors who have had mystical experiences and then read the works that immediately followed those events. This kind of text has been written for centuries.

Ancient works include the Tibetan and Egyptian Books of the Dead, which detail the experiences a soul goes through after its host body dies. The purpose of these books is not only to prepare you for death but also to imitate the experience of death so that you can be "reborn" into your own lifetime.

Medieval Europe had its share of mystics too. Especially interesting are the writings of the anchoress mystics, like Julian of Norwich, who usually wrote their greatest works after experiencing a prolonged fever or near-death experience.

More up-to-date literary simulations of the mystical experience come from authors such as James Joyce, Herman Hesse, Aldous Huxley, and poets such as William Butler Yeats or T. S. Eliot. Understanding Joyce's *Finnegan's Wake*, it is said, is as impossible as understanding the cosmos. The story is a dream, and the images used to describe that dream are taken from everywhere in literature. No one could possibly identify even a majority of the references and puns. But as Joyce would have us believe, all the information we need to decipher the text is accessible to us in the collective cultural unconscious. And indeed you will experience moments reading Joyce's masterpiece when your attempts at understanding the words disappear and your consciousness resonates in full comprehension, somewhere between yourself and the text. Try reading it aloud and it might just make sense.

13

EYES CLOSED: SLEEP, DREAMS, AND JOURNEYS

There are several ways to alter yourself that involve sleep and fantasy. These are inward journeys, where instead of looking at familiar things differently, you take your waking consciousness to unfamiliar regions. If you cannot bring Muhammad to the mountain . . .

The trick with any of the techniques in this chapter is to stay conscious. Most of us have probably had lucid dreams, experiential visualizations, and even out-of-body experiences, but have not remembered them. You cannot really consider them highs if you experienced them while you were asleep and then woke up with no memory that they ever happened. The technique to develop is to be able to watch what you are doing. You become two people at once: a participant and an observer. Ideally as a dreamer, you should gain the ability to behave consciously. For example, if you are in a dream being chased by bad guys, and you know you are having a dream, you can jump out the window and fly away. Or you can decide to grow six feet taller and beat them up. Similarly if you can follow yourself consciously as you move into an out-of-body experience, you can learn to direct your travels and go anywhere you wish.

The techniques in this chapter, then, are not highs. They do not change your waking state of consciousness. Rather, they allow you to move your consciousness into new regions. Once there, you are open to an immense range of possible actions, feelings, and landscapes. You are free to travel into different dimensions of reality. Instead of altering your mind to see the everyday world differently, you leave the mind alone and go into different space.

LUCID DREAMING

The sleep state is the most accessible of the altered states. We get there almost every night of our lives. Still, to most of us, the eight or so hours we spend in bed are like wasted time. We awake refreshed, but remember almost nothing. It is relatively easy to gain conscious access to the sleep state. There are a number of books and tapes designed to help you remember your dreams and then to behave consciously within them. Most of these methods work, with a little discipline on your part.

The foremost expert in the field of lucid dreaming is Stephen LaBerge. To do any dreamwork before reading his *Lucid Dreams* would be inefficient. He has mapped it all out already. Tapes are also available that help you to remember and take part in your dreams. The ones that worked best for us were the subliminal tapes called *Lucid Dreaming: Awaken to Your Inner Self*, put out by Yes! Technologies, 16 Finalee Avenue, Asheville, North Carolina 28803. The tapes are not a necessary component here, but, if nothing else, they heighten your awareness as you are going to sleep that you have a purpose in mind.

The tapes are part of a simple program that gives subliminal suggestions that when you hear a certain sound, you will spontaneously begin to dream lucidly. You play the suggestion tapes during the day, then at night you play a special tape on an auto-reverse cassette deck. This technique worked for us after about a week, but we found we had little control over our own actions in our dreams. We were conscious that we were dreaming, but were not free to move around. Still, the dreams we had were amazingly vivid, if not altogether lucid. (We realize this last comment raises a myriad of questions about dream morality. For example, should we even try to have control over our dreams? Aren't they an expression of our subconscious, which should be left alone? Maybe. But to us, the fun of lucid dreaming is to get to play inside your fantasies. You can still have other dreams for your sub-conscious mind's sake.)

The first step in learning to have lucid dreams on your own is to start remembering your dreams. The way to do this is to choose to do so. Before you go to sleep, tell yourself you are going to remember your dreams. Keep a pad next to your bed, and whenever you wake up, discipline yourself to write down whatever you have been dreaming. If you just cannot remember, at least write down how you feel—this might allow you to recall the source of those feelings.

Once you have a fairly good recall of your evening's dreams, you can begin the process of moving into them consciously. You can do this in either of two ways. Both of them involve recognizing the fact that you are dreaming without waking up. This in-between place is the lucid dream. They say lucid dreams occur most often in morn-ing REM (rapid eye movement) sleep. The method of exploiting morning sleep time is simple. When you first wake up, actively remember what you just dreamed. Go through the location and characters in your mind until you know the world of the dream very well. Then go back to sleep, telling yourself that when you see this world again, you will know it is a dream. Do it the same way you might remind yourself that the moment you start to make the coffee in the morning, you will remember that you have to make a certain phone call. You may not reenter the same exact dream, but chances are you will recognize it as a dream. Do this and experiment until you can play inside your dreams. If you take too extreme an action—one that does not fit in the world of the dream—you might tend to wake yourself up. You must learn how to maintain the dream state without breaking it up.

Another way of entering your dreams consciously is to work at it as you go to sleep. This is the way that has worked best for us. As we enter the state between waking and sleeping, we begin to imagine walking or moving. As a child, our friend, Seth, used to imagine running down the aisles of a huge toy store and watching all the items pass by in his peripheral vision. He would keep running until it did not even feel as if he was running anymore, but rather gliding or even flying. The wall of the toy store would open in front of him, and he would fly through all sorts of tunnels, skies, and canyons. If he could keep conscious through all this, he would end up having marvelously lucid dreams.

We think anyone could imitate this process by consciously fantasizing during the falling-asleep time. As you let go more and more, you get closer and closer to the dream state. Just hold on to one of your senses consciously—such as sight—and you will have a conscious window into your dream. The problem is you tend to fall into sleep after the dream and then forget the whole thing. There are easy ways of combatting this problem. Try setting a gentle alarm (the music option on a clock radio) to go off maybe ten minutes into the process. If you have a snooze bar, this should keep you waking up every ten minutes. Better yet, have a partner hit the snooze bar for you so that you do not even have to move. The music will gently remind you not to fall completely into sleep. After three or four of these cycles, wake up and record your experience. This same process would work well for many people at the prime-launch-window hours of early morning.

You should keep a good journal of your dream experiences. This is one of the only ways to get better at dreaming—that is, to get deeper and deeper access through the dreaming state of consciousness. Through dreams we can communicate with parts of ourselves and perhaps with other people and entities altogether. But the only way to travel down this road is by documenting and mapping out where we have gone already. By recognizing patterns in our dreams over, say, a two-year period, we can get a much better sense of where we are going, and of how to get there more efficiently. The best sourcebook we know of on how to get the most out of your dreams is *The Jungian-Senoi Dreamwork Manual*, by Strephon Kaplan-Williams (Berkeley: Journey Press, 1980—available through Journey Press, P.O. Box 9036, Berkeley, California 94709). This workbook outlines everything you ever wanted to know about dreaming but were afraid to ask. He goes into little detail on lucid dreaming itself, but his comments on how to interpret your dream symbols, as well as how to approach your dreams openly yet systematically, are indispensable to the purposeful dreamer.

When you work with the manual, you realize that every dream is a trip outside the time-space continuum. Dreams have the same shape as sex or a near-death experience. You "die" into the dream and are reborn out of it, able to live your life as a new person. Each night of your life can be the most intense experience you have ever passed through, and you will still get a good night's sleep.

VISUALIZATION

Visualizations can be used for any purpose. Their most dramatic function has been to aid in the healing of cancer victims, who visualize the cells of their body fighting and destroying cancer cells. People such as Dr. Bernie Siegal (*Love, Medicine, Miracles*) have written on the ability of people to self-heal through creative imagery. Most common are visualizations that help people relax. Even if people cannot heal themselves directly, they can at least break the cycle of being sick, getting tense, and becoming sicker. Our interest in visualizations, though, is how to use them to reach noticeably new states of consciousness.

While it is important to remove the connotations of the visualizing process as exclusively a healing technique, it is also important to distinguish between visualizations and affirmations. Affirmations are a way of trying to make something true that either is not true or that you cannot see as true. People who are experiencing their lives as impoverished, for example, might tell themselves an affirmation every morning such as: "I have all the money I need. I am a magnet for money." They may also "visualize" themselves as being very rich, or driving an expensive car, or living in a mansion. Eventually, the image the person imagines and reality are supposed to meet. We do not think this is the case. Every time you repeat an affirmation to yourself such as "I am a beautiful person," you are actually communicating the opposite. What you really hear and feel is, "I need to tell myself I am a beautiful person, because I am not." The affirmation is something outside yourself that is supposed to feed your self-image. This is impossible. All it does is accentuate the difference between where you are and where you want to be. If you want to do visualizations of this kind, the best book is Shakti Gawain's *Creative Visualization*. Many people feel they have benefited from this work; it has nothing to do with getting high.

Being high depends on you being exactly how and where you want to be at a given moment. Getting high means getting free of time-space. When you are high, you do not need to remind yourself of anything. Visualizations that get you high work by releasing the mind. They become like dreams, where the rules of reality no longer hold. They may bring you deeper into the workings of your body, or even bring you out of your body altogether.

Visualizations are really just organized, sometimes preplanned, fantasies. A person lies down, closes his eyes, and then listens to a tape or to another person who is guiding him through an imagined experience. Therapists use this technique to help patients get over problems by accessing their subconscious creativity. The subconscious is allowed to communicate with the conscious mind. For example, a therapist might say, "You find an envelope. Inside the envelope is a note. Who is the note from?" The patient may answer, "It's from my father." The therapist responds, "Read the note." You get the idea. It is a directed free association.

We can direct the visualization any way we want. We can even direct it ourselves, if we are not embarrassed to fantasize. In any case, with a little practice we can bring ourselves, through imagery, into a desired state of consciousness. In the acting profession, this technique is called sense memory. To feel a certain way, an actor will remember what he was seeing, smelling, hearing, tasting, or touching during some event in his life when he felt that way. After he has accurately recalled these sensations and concentrated on them, he will usually begin to feel the same way. By visualizing sensations we have never experienced, though, we can also bring our consciousness into states we have never experienced.

The easy way to start doing visualizations is to buy prerecorded ones on tape. The first one that comes to mind is a very bizarre one called *The Cauldron of Thoth* available through Nicki Scully, P.O. Box 5025, Eugene, Oregon 97405. It has a pretty pagan feeling about it, but it takes you through an out-of-body experience, as well as introducing you to some of the characters in Egyptian mythology. There's also some pretty cool music. You can also find lots of less intense visualization tapes at any New Age bookstore. Just make sure not to get any tape that is *for* something in particular. Most of these cassettes are sold as visualizations to quit smoking or to lose weight. Just get one that says it is for a good time or for general relaxation.

Another great source of visualizations is the *Anthology of Imagery Techniques*, edited by Anees A. Sheikh, Ph.D. This tome contains dozens of visualizations, as well as ways to use them.

The best technique for doing prepared visualizations is to record them on tape, then listen to them. Be sure to leave time to imagine whatever you are narrating. For example, if you are reciting, "You come to a stone wall . . . you see a man sitting on top . . . you walk up to the man . . ." be sure to leave pauses during which you will be able to imagine what the wall and man look like. You can also have a friend read one to you, or take turns reading them to each other.

It helps to set up an atmosphere conducive to the energy of fantasy. Burn candles and incense, turn the lights low, and play some evocative music.

Here is a sample of a visualization that can get you high:

Your body is heavy . . . it is one with the earth . . . you can feel the gravity the earth exerts on you . . . you can feel the gravity you exert on the earth . . . you are lying in an open field . . . the sun is bright above you . . . but there is also a cool breeze . . . the air is sweet and delicious . . . you can feel the

*cool green grass beneath you . . . you can touch it with your
hands . . . you look up into the sky . . . it is blue except for the
sun directly above you . . .*

*With each breath in and out, your awareness of the planet be-
neath you grows . . . it is most definitely round . . . it is most
definitely moving . . . you are on your back, in the middle of a
field, on a whirling sphere . . . the movement is
delightful . . . you feel the blood in your body come to the surface
of your skin from the motion . . . enjoy the sensation . . .*

*You get curious about the world around you . . . you look
around . . . there are trees at the edge of the field . . . you decide
to get up to investigate, and the moment you make the decision, you
feel your body begin to rise by itself . . . your head rises first, followed by your body . . . you are completely vertical, and still
rising . . . as you rise, you look around yourself . . . see the
trees . . . past the trees are little towns . . . past the towns are
lakes, rivers, bridges . . . you rise higher and higher . . . you
can see the curving of the earth . . . the circular horizon . . .*

*As you rise, you begin to feel warm . . . you are closer to the
sun . . . but inside you, too, there is a warmth . . . a fire seems
to be burning inside you, propelling your motion upward like the
engines of a rocket ship . . . you get hotter and hotter . . . your
face becomes flushed . . . it is a beautiful, encompassing
warmth . . . you are heated inside and out . . . you rise with
amazing speed . . .*

You feel warm most of all in the center of your chest . . . it

feels as if there were an ice cube deep in the middle of your chest
being melted . . . as the ice cube melts, it turns to water . . . the
water diffuses throughout your body . . . your whole consciousness
is in this ice cube now . . . you feel yourself melting away into
liquid . . . your body seems to drop away as you become just water and heat . . . flame and liquid, rising into the sky . . .

The water becomes so warm that it turns to vapor, bringing
you into the air as steam . . . the fire drops away back to the
earth, which is miles and miles below you . . . you are just
vapor . . . you spread out into the air . . . you are one with the
air . . . you diffuse throughout the atmosphere . . . you are em-
bracing the earth as air . . . you feel cool and sweet as air
itself . . . you have no weight . . . you have no form . . . you
are air . . .

You continue to flow outward . . . it is no longer getting
brighter . . . the sky is actually getting darker and
cooler . . . the earth has become a small sphere within you as you
continue to move out . . . you are moving out into
space . . . you are air, diffusing into space . . .

You move outward in all directions at once . . . you move
beyond air . . . you are lighter and lighter . . . smoother and
smoother . . . you are moving into the absolute textureless
dark . . . there is no feeling, no direction . . . just
movement . . . float . . . enjoy . . .

When you want to, realize that the blackness around you is the
inside of a huge body . . . fill the void of this huge, human body

*with your consciousness . . . fill its legs . . . fill its
hands . . . fill its abdomen . . . fill its chest . . . fill its
head . . . bring warmth and life to this new body . . . .*

*Enjoy the feeling of weight . . . this new body is lying on
the ground . . . lying on the cool grass . . . look around
you . . . you are back in the warm field . . . the sun is still directly above you . . . the cool breeze blows against your
face . . . you are where you were.*

*Take time to rest before slowly opening your eyes, stretching,
and sitting up.*

We have found that the best way to do visualizations is
freestyle. Just lie down in the same way and imagine what
you want to. You do not need to put it into words. Just
visualize whatever kind of journey you want to take, and
take it.

OUT-OF-BODY TRAVEL

Out-of-body experiences are not everyday events—at least
not for most of us. The first and still the foremost
out-of-body adventurer in the modern scientific community is Robert A. Monroe, whose book *Journeys Out of the
Body* and its sequel, *Far Journeys* are the best documenta-
tion available on the subject.

Mystics, awakened teachers, and shamans go out-of-body regularly, but usually as the result of a talent they are born with. They can tell you stories about the places they have gone and the entities they have met, but cannot really share the process by which they get out of the physical body. They just do—this is why they are shamans. Occasionally someone of a normal background has a spontaneous journey out-of-body. It could be during an intense meditation, while going to sleep, during an accident, or just during nothing special at all.

Most people react to an out-of-body experience as a fantasy. They cannot believe it really happened. It is so out of place with physical reality that they assume it was a hallucination, and they don't tell anyone. Robert Monroe responded differently. He realized that during the night he was actually traveling outside of his body. He wrote his first book about these experiences, then set up the Monroe Institute of Applied Sciences to study out-of-body travel.

Since then he has trained thousands of people to get out of their bodies for varying periods of time. The "traveler" lies in bed in one room, in voice contact with a "monitor," who watches the vital signs of the voyager from a control console down the hall. It's like a science fiction movie, except that the results are real. Monroe developed recordings of tones at frequencies that get people into a state of consciousness where they are physically asleep yet mentally awake. It is from this state that the person can get out-of-body.

Monroe has made these sounds available on tape. His Hemi-Sync cassettes, like the tapes of Brother Charles, work through hemispheric alignment. A catalog is available from the Institute, located in Faber, Virginia (804-361-1500). You can get started with a set of cassettes that should run you about $30. If you intend to get out-of-body, this is the way to begin. For a more hands-on experience, you can take a week-long workshop at the Institute itself. The starter course, including room and board, should run you about $1,000. From our contact with the Institute, we can honestly say they are not scammers. These people believe in what they are saying, love what they are doing, and want to share it with as many people as possible. It is not a business but a research center.

The research they have done is amazing. They are uncovering a map of the universe that has nothing to do with the galaxies we know about. They explore inner space—or is it true other space?—and accurately document everything they find. They have contacted dozens of kinds of entities and found many, many different realms of existence. They are coming to understand everything from reincarnation to the nature of life itself. The out-of-body explorers who work at the Institute make even the most earnest channeling look like a parlor game.

Monroe outlined in his first book a way to get out-of-body, but admitted in his second book that the approach does not work for all people all the time. Getting out-of-body is not as simple as he first believed. Nonetheless the technique has worked for many people, and even if you do not get complete satisfaction, it is probably still the best preliminary training with which to begin.

Monroe breaks up the learning process into three major steps: relaxation, vibration, and separation. To get properly relaxed, you need to be able to recognize and exploit a sleeping body with an awake mind. You are first to practice this exercise at bedtime. Get to the place where you feel yourself dozing off, and, without moving, keep your mind alert by concentrating on one thing. Stay in this state for as long as possible. Once you can do this, see if you can stay in this state without concentrating on one thing in particular. Many thoughts and impressions from the day will appear to you when you are in this state. Let them all pass until you just see black. This could take a week or so.

After you can do this, attempt to get into the same state when you are not tired. This is tricky, but not impossible. Monroe suggests trying this upon waking from the night's sleep, or after a nap, so that your body is still relaxed.

Monroe next talks about a vibrational state. This is as far as we have gotten with his technique. Monroe advises removing any and all possible distractions (telephone, roommates, etc.) and lying in a semidark room. You are to hold yourself in the deepest state of relaxation you can while breathing through a half-open mouth. Next you are to stare out at the darkness immediately in front of you, then extend the point of focus slowly farther away, until it is about six feet from you. Then let the point of focus rise directly upward. After you sense the vibrational energy at that point, let it move closer until it is directly above your head. Bring the vibration down into your head by "reaching" for it. Next Monroe suggests acclimating to the vibrational state by speeding it up. You turn it from a slightly uncomfortable buzz into a smoother sensation, or almost no sensation at all.

Finally, to get out-of-body, you are to get to the state of vibration and practice reaching for objects with your "second body." You should reach for things "as if," but not actually stretch your arm toward it. Your eyes are closed, so it does not matter what you reach for. If you do this right, you will touch things that are physically out of your reach. You are even supposed to be able to reach through them to other things. To get all the way out-of-body, get into the vibrational state, maintaining absolute control of your thought process. Imagine how nice it would be to float up and out of your body and your "second body" should take the hint. To get back, you are simply to recall what it would be like to be lying on the bed again. You open your eyes only after you have gotten back inside.

This is an extremely condensed version of Monroe's instructions, designed to give you an idea of his process. It is not a substitute for buying his book and following his lesson plan. He travels out-of-body, we do not.

Better yet, since Monroe admits that even his instructions are in some ways incomplete, contact the Institute and buy a set of tapes. They are designed to bring you well into the vibrational state without much work on your part. People have been reported to go out-of-body on their first exposure to Monroe's Hemi-Sync cassettes.

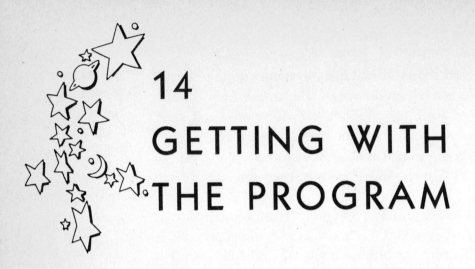

14
GETTING WITH
THE PROGRAM

This chapter describes a wide variety of types of dedication. If you take almost anything in nature, contemplate it, and dedicate yourself to it, you will experience a great high. If you have ever been in love, you will understand this phenomenon. Finding anything, even an insight, that rings absolutely true can resonate as ecstasy for quite a long while. If a person finds Jesus, for example, the initial divine pleasure of "being saved" will be reexperienced every Sunday at church. At each new service resonating frequencies are added to the initial striking of the bell, so that eventually everything in life moves with divine ecstasy.

There are many devotional systems in the world today. Most of them would resent categorization of this sort, but this is what religion is, and why it works. There is nothing wrong with it. We have also included in this chapter the more modern sorts of programming. Again, these are peak experiences that produce highs and are later confirmed and expanded upon in subsequent seminars or workshops. All of these programs begin with a spark of truth—or at least one in the shape of truth—that ignites as a full flame in a human being. It's not important what the particular dogma is, so long as it does not call for you to hurt anyone. The downfall of almost all these programs is that they invite addiction. Most practitioners of a faith or self-help organization will never shun your interest or dedication, no matter how obsessive it becomes.

It feels good to be in love with anything. Loving something and devoting yourself to it feels very comforting. Don't let this feeling fool you into devoting yourself to something dangerous. Here are a few groups in which membership feels good and the downsides are fairly minimal.

EST AND THE SEMINAR PHENOMENON

Est was one of the first of the seminar programs. Originally it consisted of a two-weekend "training" in which a leader with a microphone stood on a stage in front of a hundred or so people and brought them to the realization that they were in control of their experience. The principal purpose of the est training was to change your experience of life so that the situations you had been putting up with or trying to change would clear up in the process of living. We did the est training and found it to be quite positive. Despite the est clones and est jargon, Werner Erhard's concepts proved a valuable first lesson in how to use experience to move forward rather than getting stuck. "Getting it" meant getting nothing and everything. It meant understanding that "getting it" is a state of mind. If you chose to be a person who "got it," you were. There were many useful concepts in the est training, which, more than anything else, helped people realize that they were the only ones responsible for their experience of life.

The problem was that many est graduates experienced a high on leaving the original training but then lost the effect. Their lives seemed to return to their original states. To combat this, the est people created the Seminar

Program, a relatively inexpensive way to "recharge" the est experience once a week. The Seminar Program still exists today.

But what happened to the est training? It was "retired" and replaced with something called the Forum. The ideas of est were new in the seventies, but already fairly integrated into American culture by the eighties. Most of the people who were going to take the training already had, and those who had not pretty well understood the principle of self as source. The Forum is the new introduction into the est community and is offered in most cities. Scandal has forced Erhard to sell the organization to his associates and the future of this work is uncertain.

We have mixed feelings about est. It can be a valuable experience in many ways. It can certainly get you high for several weeks and then provide you with a community of like-minded people in which to regenerate your experience. The problems lie in the organization's constant pressure on its members to find new trainees. Spreading the word becomes the word. In a devotional sense this is fine. Sharing information is one of the only things worth doing with it. Still, if your main obstacle to being high is psychological or conceptual, the est seminars are a relatively painless catharsis, which can clear the way for you to move on to bigger and better things.

In the same basic category as est would be seminar

programs such as the Insight Seminars or Robert Fritz's Institute for Human Evolution and his program Technologies for Creating. Not all of these suffer from the same problems as est, but the majority do suffer from the problem—as do most churches—of having their greatest followers be the most needy people. It seems that the strong move on and out, whereas the weaker stay behind and move up within the organization. The best way to find the right program for you is to talk to friends who have completed one of these seminars. There is really nothing in any of them that could screw you up, although they all cost in the hundreds of dollars to try. Still, nearly all of the seminars make you feel really good for a while, and they do provide you with some lasting tools to make your life work for you rather than against you. Just keep in mind that the attachments you lose can just as easily be replaced by the programs that alleviated them.

A COURSE IN MIRACLES

This started as a book but has developed into a network of study groups throughout the world. A Course in Miracles was channeled by a group of psychologists. It is a profoundly rich assessment of the human condition and the path to awakening. To follow the program, all you really need to do is buy the book and follow the instructions. There are many teachers—some qualified and some not so qualified—who work with the books to help others through the course. You can do it this way, but you do not have to. The book is designed for anyone to use.

It should take at least a year to get through the entire course, and then you will probably want to start over again, or else continue with your favorite exercises. Ultimately A Course in Miracles takes the rest of your life, but throughout, you will gain a great number of insights into the practical ramifications of karma, spirituality, and different levels of awareness. A Course in Miracles provides you with a direct experience of why you are here, where you came from, where you are going, and what to do about it. Truly understanding all this necessitates an alteration of consciousness.

RIGHT ACTION

Most of the major religions were developed to preserve the teachings of awakened people. Buddhism, for example, did not arise until many years after Buddha's death, when his followers decided to record what had happened. Similarly while Christ was alive, there was no need for

Christianity; the awakened teacher was walking among us, and all we needed to do was follow him.

With or without an awakened teacher, you still have the ability to experience the bliss of his presence. As explained in the chapter on meditation, one way to experience bliss is to contemplate a person or deity to whom you are devoted. If you see this being as perfect, your love will grow. You will eventually see the object of your devotion manifest in everything around you. The world becomes a manifestation of the Buddha, the Christ, or the guru of your choice. This can also be done with an idea. For example, you may realize one day that everything is light. "There is nothing else but light. Everything that seems to be something other than light is actually light, but appears to be something different because I cannot yet see it as light." Slowly this awareness permeates your consciousness, and you are in a long-lasting subtly altered state.

The best way to experience a devotional high is through action. You yourself become a manifestation of the deity or idea through your actions. For example, many devout Christians end up working in missions in the worst parts of town. A manifestation of the perfection of Christ is for his followers to put his compassion into practice.

Handing out food at a shelter for homeless people is a deeply rewarding experience, not just because it relieves you of your feelings of guilt for being in a better socio-economic position. The process itself is a manifestation of a type of compassion. You are acknowledging one of your deepest needs: to help others. This can take a variety of forms—working in a hospital, an orphanage, an old-age home—but the high is the same in all of these cases. It comes from sharing.

Many people choose to share in less immediately tangible ways. Jehovah's Witnesses and Mormons, for example, go door-to-door sharing their gospel. Other people use their time off to teach illiterate people how to read and write. Even professional healing techniques—such as Mariel and Reichian—are practices of a devotional discipline. In any of these cases the giver is a person who believes strongly in the value of what he or she has to offer. Watching someone else benefit confirms this value and feels good.

It sounds too simple to get high by doing nice things for people, but it works, especially if you feel you are manifesting some kind of truth. Your actions become an extension of something much bigger than yourself. You are only a conduit for a greater energy, which, as it flows through you on its way to helping others, gets you remarkably high.

15

LESS IS MORE: GETTING HIGH BY DOING WITHOUT

Many religions advocate self-deprivation. Monks of most faiths are told at one time or another to fast, take vows of silence, cut themselves off from the world, practice celibacy, or even wear patches over their eyes. These techniques are employed as teaching tools. A nun who does not talk for a year may learn, for example, how she has always used speech in order to feed her ego rather than to help others. A monk who takes a vow of celibacy may gain an understanding that, for him, sex has been wasting vital life energy. By fasting one might learn self-discipline and be better prepared for the perils of the spiritual journey he or she hopes to take. (Some monks practiced fasting so that they would be able to meditate for weeks at a time without worrying about food.)

Our interest in self-deprivation, however, has nothing to do with such goals. While exploiting some of the techniques developed over the ages, the techniques outlined below are listed for the exclusive purpose of providing you access to altered states of consciousness. Do not fool yourself that you are fasting for better health or depriving yourself of speech to make up for lies you have told. Keep your head out of this.

Self-deprivation forces your mind to rebalance itself. Our states of consciousness are dependent upon our perceptions of reality; they can even be defined as such. By altering the manner in which we perceive reality, we alter the state of our consciousness. The result of self-deprivation is to alter the total picture of reality by removing one or two pieces of it. A world with no news reports or media is extremely different from one with a radio blasting the headlines twenty-four hours a day. We have gotten very used to the stimuli that surround us, so much so that we have become deadened. Depriving ourselves of just one of the elements of the perceptual landscape to which we have become accustomed will necessitate a reactivation of our learning centers. With the

mind busy testing the new environment, the consciousness is freed to roam around and play.

Self-deprivation is not a form of penance. It is a
temporary closure, which allows other things to open.
Often we shut our eyes in order to think more clearly.
With unwanted stimuli removed, the mind no longer
needs to act like a filtering system. More brain "bytes" can
be put to work on the real problem at hand.

One of the principal challenges to pursuing the path
to spiritual awakening is called the peripheral attack. This
takes the form of distractions. The only reason distractions
take hold is because the person views himself as somehow
separate from that which is around him. To the enlightened individual the self and the world are the same. He
experiences a great unity of consciousness. This is the
"oneness" spoken about in spiritual texts. Since we are not
yet awakened people, we need to eliminate the possibility
of distractions so that we do not blame our problems on
things that seem to be out of our control. The most
common obstacles to a desired state of consciousness—a
high—are the peripheral distractions of everyday life.
When you remove a component of everyday life, you also
remove a battery of distractions you may never have
realized were holding you down.

Self-deprivations do not "deprive" us, they free us.
They remove external influences so that we can experience

our inner states more subtly. A common misconception about the Jewish holiday Yom Kippur is that the day's fast is some sort of penance. It is not. The Jews fast on their day of atonement so that they can more fully concentrate on their prayers. Similarly, by experiencing any self-deprivation, we free ourselves to concentrate on what we want to focus on.

In any period of self-deprivation you will experience moments of great intensity. It is precisely at these moments, however, that the potential for great alterations of consciousness exists. With each threshold of discomfort comes the opportunity for greater clarity. Still, you must use care and judgment. Most deprivations work best under supervision. Find a friend who knows you well and whose orders you promise to follow. When your friend says you have had enough, quit whatever deprivation you are trying.

The easiest deprivations are the ones that take the shortest amount of time and do not involve any vital bodily function such as eating or sleeping. But with any of the following techniques it is important that you take ample time to prepare and then even more time to recover.

FLOTATION TANKS

Developed by John Lilly and later made famous in the film *Altered States,* flotation tanks are the easiest way to explore deprivation as a method of getting high. Flotation tanks are dark boxes filled with very salty water. You go inside, shut the lid, and float on your back (the salt allows you to do this effortlessly) in total darkness and silence. Except for the feeling of warm water against your head and back, you receive no neural stimuli.

The theory here is that with no external influences you are free to experience your internal state. You begin to hear the tones that resonate within your head all the time but are usually drowned out by other noises. In the blackness your optic nerves are free to discharge stored energy in the form of hallucinations. Your body is free to experience the sensations that it generates by itself, freed of gravity and muscular effort.

It may take a little while to get used to the sensation of being in a tank. The water level tends to end up near your ears, and it might be uncomfortable for you to let water inside them. If you think this will be the case, bring comfortable earplugs. This will also eliminate the influence of the sound of the water moving around in your ears if you bob up and down. We also recommend eating lightly or not at all before floating. You do not want to spend your entire session listening to your food digest or feeling it move through your alimentary canal.

Most reasonably sized towns have places that rent flotation tanks on an hourly basis. Check New Age publications or inquire at a New Age bookshop. Find the most reputable center around and follow the instructor's advice exactly. If there is nowhere to float near you and you have your heart set on this method, you can buy plans for a tank, a tank kit, or even a fully assembled tank for use in your own home. You can purchase one through the Samadhi Tank Company, 2123 Lake Shore Drive, Los Angeles, California 90039. We would not recommend purchasing one until you are sure you want to invest real time in this path. The last thing you need is an unused float tank in your garage. If you do purchase your own, read the manufacturer's instructions carefully.

The best source of information about floating is Michael Hutchinson's *The Book of Floating: Exploring the Private Sea* ($9.95 through Mega Brain, 1375 Sutter Street, Suite 402, San Francisco, California 94109). But the most daring explorer of tanks and their associated states of consciousness is still John Lilly, who documented his work most successfully in *The Deep Self.* This book even has plans for tanks in its appendix, as well as valuable experiments to try during tank sessions. But be forewarned: Lilly's experiments often involve psychedelics. The experiences he describes were a combination of sensory deprivation and ketamine experimentation. Still, much of what Lilly experienced in the tank is available to us without taking drugs. If you are journeying within to see what's inside, then do that. If you take drugs before going into the tank, you are not looking at yourself but at your drugged self. There is a big difference. The point of deprivation is to remove influences, not to introduce them. Go into the tank with as little as possible and your mind will expand naturally and effortlessly. What you will see is what is really there.

At first most people experience only a great relaxation. (This can take a while, as most people first become acutely aware of their own body sounds and phosphene discharge.) Then thoughts about other things slowly enter consciousness. When this happens, remind yourself that you are inside a tank and that there is nothing but you. The problems of your day may move into your consciousness, but you must realize that they are not acting upon you in the tank. Anything you are not experiencing at this moment is not real. It is memory. It is a story. Your presence in the tank is the only reality. External influences can only affect you by your own choice. In the tank it does not matter who is president or to whom you are married. You have the opportunity to be free of everything, from light and sound to your job and your financial status. The only thing left is your consciousness.

It is very difficult to shut off the internal chatter of thoughts. We usually live under such stress that it is difficult to do anything in a tank except release thought. This incessant internal monologue may never fade away. Do not try to suppress it. Let it rattle on as long as it wants. Just slowly stop paying attention. Whenever you realize you are involved in an internal monologue, just say to yourself, "Blah-blah-blah." Acknowledge that your mind needs to talk and let it. Your real consciousness, however, need not be involved.

Imagine, for example, that your mind and your consciousness are both in the same huge room. See your mind as a little radio in the corner somewhere that was left on. (Worse yet, it wasn't even left on music, but on an AM all-talk station.) There is no way to turn the radio off, so just leave it alone. Look around at other parts of the room. Find doors, push through walls, or do whatever you want. You probably get the point. The mind may rattle on forever. Do not worry about it. Listen if you like, but when you get bored, simply float away. You can catch up with what your mind is saying when you get back, the same way that you can understand a soap opera even after a month of not watching.

Eventually—it may not be your first or even your

fifth float session when this happens—you will move out of the mind's jurisdiction. You will experience the infinite possibility of a world with no sights, sounds, or sensations. You will have the experience of being asleep when fully conscious. You may even begin to travel out-of-body or out of the time-space continuum.

Space has nothing to do with area, distance, or volume. There is just as much space within you as outside of you. And for inward journeys you don't need to involve NASA or huge cash reserves. Lilly has described dozens of levels of consciousness he has reached on his journeys inward, and labeled them by number. On each of the different levels there are different personalities one can meet. These are "aliens" of a different sort: conscious beings who live interdimensionally rather than "out there" somewhere. We will surely document our interactions with these beings long before we develop the technology to reach out into outer space to find other inhabited planets at our own level of reality.

But getting high in an isolation tank is a much easier proposition than developing a relationship with an interdimensional being. All you need to do is learn how to move past the emissions of your normally overworked senses. Once you learn to shorten the initial period of disorientation and sensory discharge, you will move into a

deeply relaxed yet extremely clear state of awareness. You
have to try this to understand what we mean.

NO TALKING

Try not to speak for a week. Create a situation where this
is feasible, such as at a retreat or even at a motel in some
beautiful place. Bring a paper and pencil with you and
write a note telling the proprietor you cannot speak. Then
do whatever you want without talking to anyone.

In the strictest sense a vow of silence is not really a
deprivation. You are not deprived of food, light, or
information. The only thing you lose is the ability to
express yourself and your intentions. But by depriving
yourself of something as simple as speech, you take the
first step in losing your ego. If you give up the need to
communicate, you are no longer inflicting your own will
on other people.

After even one day a feeling of extreme satisfaction
will come over you. Unable to manipulate other people,
you will lose the urge to control things. Concepts such as
"needs" and "self" disappear. You may begin to smile for
no reason.

NO NEWS IS GOOD NEWS

Another simple yet profound deprivation is a media blackout. Do whatever you have to to stay ignorant of world events. Avoid stories of all kinds. The only things you should talk about or listen to must involve your immediate experience. Nothing else matters or exists.

This is more difficult than it sounds. You must avoid television, radio, newspapers, magazines, and the printed word of almost any kind other than maps or directions for something. Harder still is to avoid talking about things other than the present moment. It is nearly impossible to go to work without hearing somebody talk about a famous trial or plane crash. You cannot hear this kind of information. It is even more difficult to keep yourself from getting involved in conversations about stories. Even telling a stranger what you do for a living is a story. Your profession, unless you are engaged in it at the precise moment, has nothing to do with your interaction with a stranger you meet in the park. The rules in this deprivation are demanding but clear-cut. Do not speak about or listen to anything other than the moment.

The longer you can keep this up, the better. Enough time needs to pass so that it really feels as if the world has kept spinning without your knowledge. Governments may have changed hands, AT&T may have lost its monopoly over the phone system, the president may have sent troops to Burma, and nuclear fusion may have revealed God. Unless it happens in your field of vision, it is immaterial. Out of sight, out of mind is your way of life.

Remarkable changes in your attitude toward life take place in just a few days. Some people experience an alteration in consciousness after just six hours of not consulting their answering machines. A commodities trader would probably find this deprivation exercise impossible. But even for those of us who are not compulsively tied to stories, disconnection from the global drama is a remarkably freeing experience. Dropping out, so to speak, opens a whole new world of directly experiential living.

One of the easiest ways to undergo a media deprivation is to travel cross-country. Hop in the car with some cash, a credit card, and a pretty partner if you can find one and just go. The difference between this and a normal vacation is that you are not just vacationing from a place or a job but from everything. All that is left is the process by which you experience life. Nothing you have ever done or plan to do matters. You become nothing but your experience. After a day or so of catharsis (similar to the discharges of sound and light you experience in a flotation tank) you will begin to feel the freedom that a media deprivation affords.

It will not be boring. On the contrary, your senses will become so heightened that everything will seem as though you are experiencing it for the first time. Instead of looking at things, classifying them, and moving on, you will begin to look just for looking's sake. There is no longer a storehouse of information. There is no reason to remember anything, because there is no reason to repeat anything. You simply move through time and space with no memories, no cares, and no stakes. This is the ultimate vacation.

As after any intense high, you will need to reintegrate into normal life slowly. Many of the things you have been holding on to for security may seem useless when you get back. Even your job may seem pointless. Don't take any rash actions at first, until you have had time to get back into the motion of the regular world, if you choose to rejoin it.

FASTING

We think fasting is more of a physical trip than anything else, but we include it here because it is certainly the most obvious of the deprivations to try. We did not get high from not eating, we just got hungry. Still, for centuries people have been using fasting as a purification, so there is probably something to it. It seems to us that the most beneficial aspect of fasting is that it frees your body from the process of digestion and frees your mind from the concern with food. You streamline your day, release the toxins in your body, increase the sensitivity of your alimentary canal, and clarify your spiritual intentions. Your day is streamlined because ingesting and digesting food is no longer one of your concerns. Your time is no longer spent between and during meals. The day divides itself by your thoughts and activities instead. For those of you who have a fixation with eating, this is a major change of focus. Also, by clearing your insides of food, you free up many organs of your body, not to mention your bloodstream. The digestive tract is the seat of human emotion. Most stomachaches have a major psychological component. By taking food out of your system, you increase your sensitivity to the physical manifestations of your emotional states. People eat when they are upset because it quite literally numbs their insides. The stomach and intestines are given food, a new problem to deal with, so that they no longer embody your emotional life so tangibly. But without food the alimentary canal becomes more unified with your consciousness. No longer relegated to crushing and sorting out matter, these organs can listen to signals from you instead of your food. Similarly you are in a much better position to hear what your body is telling you when you have not just shoved a Snickers bar inside.

One of the subtler effects of a fast is on your ego. Eating is a taking. To eat is to sacrifice another life—however simple—in order to energize your own. There is nothing wrong in this. We have to eat to keep our consciousness functioning. But to deprive ourselves of food for a while allows us to reevaluate our position in the scheme of things. We can step out, temporarily, of the food chain and the fight for survival. We can experience what it is like to take nothing. Life is defined by its ability and effort to maintain itself. If you do not eat, you exercise conscious will over the very animal instinct that created you out of the primordial sludge. There is a simple, egoless state of consciousness associated with this realization, which is the high of fasting.

Be sure to get a checkup before undertaking a fast and follow your doctor's directions carefully. Fasting can be dangerous if not done properly.

Don't just stop eating. Your doctor will know the best kind of fast for you. The general rules are to begin slowly and end slowly. Don't have a huge meal just before you fast. This defeats the purpose. The fast works best if you eat only brown rice for a day in order to clear out your system. When you do fast, drink plenty of fluids. If you allow yourself to drink juices rather than just water, you will feel a lot better and be able to go a lot longer. When you break the fast, be sure you do it gradually. Don't just go out and eat a steak dinner. Start with some fruit or melon, then work up to simple vegetable carbohydrates.

16

STAYING HIGH

Human beings tend to experience life by means of contrasts. We know we are experiencing love if we feel sadness after our loved one is gone. We know we are happy only when we have been relieved of sadness. Similarly, to get high presupposes there is such a thing as low. This is an unfortunately limited view of the world—one that depends on duality and unworthiness in order to perpetuate itself.

Race-car drivers say they love the danger of their sport because it makes them appreciate life more. Knowing they might die tomorrow makes them value the present. In the same way many of us measure the quality of our lives by the quantity of peak experiences we can accumulate. This assumes that somehow regular life is inadequate. It is not.

It is possible to be high most or all of the time. This does not mean being disoriented or stoned. It means being extraordinarily alert and aware. As we discussed in the introduction, the mind acts like a filter for our awareness. As we feel safer and more a part of whatever life may bring to us, the less we need that filter—and the less we need to resist the natural flow of being. This flow is pure movement and pure bliss.

A "rush" is a momentary experience of the movement of the cosmos. Everything is moving all the time, but we have shut off our awareness of it. When we get momentarily high, disoriented, or free, we experience the movement. Consciousness itself is merely a movement receptor. The more movement one's consciousness opens to, the more alive it becomes. When one's consciousness becomes totally alive—that is, aware of all the movements that there are—it is fully awakened. The chaos, illusions, and attachments we cling to prevent us from experiencing true movement. We create a fiction called reality in order to limit our sense of the universe's movement. Altered states of consciousness detach us momentarily from this fictional reality and allow us to see it as illusion. This is the first step in awakening.

From the time we realize we are conscious beings, we are trying to wake up. Children spin in circles on their mother's kitchen floor to stimulate their consciousnesses with movement. People get high on drugs in an attempt to experience movement in their lives. It is not that there is a particular state of consciousness everyone gropes toward. The *alteration* of consciousness is what feels so good. The changes from one state to another are what imitate birth, death, and even enlightenment.

But getting high is only an imitation of something even more real. It is like a flight simulator. The Tibetans performed their Book of the Dead rituals as a test run for death and rebirth. Most of us who are concerned with things like reincarnation, out-of-body travel, and past-life regression are actually preoccupied with surviving our own deaths. Likewise, getting high imitates the kind of change that may occur at death. By getting high and returning to the straight world, we suggest to ourselves that we can beat death, or at least practice the process of dying.

To be high all the time would be to eliminate from your consciousness the dualities of high and straight, good and bad, mind and body, and life and death. You would no longer experience alterations of consciousness. All that would be left is the experience of movement. It would not be disorienting, because you would see how you yourself are part of this movement. You are not passively carried by the flow of movement but neither are you expending energy to keep up with it. You simply realize how you *are* the flow. The rest is a free ride.

SUGGESTED READING BY CHAPTER

Chapter 1

Andrew Weil. *The Natural Mind: A New Way of Looking at Drugs and the Higher Consciousness.* Boston: Houghton Mifflin Co., 1972.

Timothy Leary, Ralph Metzner, and Richard Alpert. *The Psychedelic Experience: A Manual Based on the Tibetan Book of the Dead.* New York: Citadel Press, 1976.

Chapter 2

Jose and Miriam Arguëlles. *Mandala*. Boston: Shambhala, 1972.

George Pennington, *Little Manual for Players of the Glass Bead Game*. Tisbury, Wiltshire, Eng. Element Books, 1983.

Carlos Castaneda. *Journey to Ixtlan*. New York: Touchstone Books, 1973.

Pierre Derlon. *Secrets Oubliés des Derniers Initiés Gitans*. Paris: Editions Robert Laffont, 1977.

Chapter 3

John Beaulieu. *Music and Sound in the Healing Arts*. Barrytown, New York: Station Hill Press, 1987.

Chapter 4

Stanislav Grof. *The Adventure of Self Discovery*. Albany: State University of New York Press, 1988.

B.K.S. Iyengar. *Light on Pranayama*. New York: Crossroad, 1985.

André van Lysebeth. *Pranayama: The Yoga of Breathing*. London: Unwin Paperbacks, 1979.

Kristin Linklater. *Freeing the Natural Voice*. New York: Drama Book Publishers, 1976.

Chapter 5

Jolan Chang. *The Tao of Love and Sex*. New York: Dutton, 1977.

Nik Douglas and Penny Slinger. *Sexual Secrets: The Alchemy of Ecstasy*. New York: Destiny Books, 1979.

Marcus Allen. *Tantra for the West*. San Rafael, Calif.: New World, 1981.

Jack Lee Rosenberg. *Total Orgasm*. New York: Random House, 1973.

Chapter 6

Ram Dass. *Journey of Awakening*. New York: Bantam Books, 1978.

David Shienkin. *Path of the Kabbalah*. New York: Paragon, 1986.

Chapter 7

Kundalini Research Institute of the 3HO Foundation. *Kundalini Yoga/Sadhana Guidlines*. New York: KRI Publications, 1978.

Jellaluddin Rumi. *Unseen Rain*. Translated by Coleman Barks and John Moyne. Putney, Vt.: Threshold Books, 1986.

Jou Tsung Hwa, *The Tao of Tai-chi Chuan*. Rutland, Vt.: Charles E. Tuttle Co., 1983.

Chapter 8

James F. Fixx. *The Complete Book of Running*. New York: Random House, 1977.

Chapter 10

Findhorn Community. *The Findhorn Garden*. New York: Harper and Row, 1975.

Chapter 11

Rosemany Feitis. *Ida Rolf Talks About Rolfing and Physical Reality*. Boulder: Rolf Institute, 1978.

Ed and Judy Colbert. *The Spa Guide*. Chester, Conn.: The Globe Pequot Press, 1988.

Chapter 12

Ellman, Richard. *James Joyce*. Oxford: Oxford University Press, 1959.

Herman Hesse. *Magister Ludi: The Glass Bead Game*. New York: Bantam, 1970.

Daniel Goleman. *The Meditative Mind*. Los Angeles: Jeremy P. Tarcher, Inc., 1977.

Isshu Miura and Ruth Fuller Sasaki. *The Zen Koan*. San Diego: Harcourt Brace Jovanovich, 1965.

Paul Reps. *Zen Flesh, Zen Bones*. New York: Doubleday, various years.

Idries Shah. *The Way of the Sufi*. New York: Dutton, 1970.

Perle Epstein. *Kabbalah: The Way of the Jewish Mystic*. Boston: Shambhala, 1978.

Z'ev ben Shimon Halevi. *Kabbalah: Tradition and Hidden Knowledge*. London: Thames and Hudson, 1979.

Z'ev ben Shimon Halevi. *The Way of the Kabbalah*. New York: Random House, 1974.

Steven Forrest. *The Inner Sky*. San Diego: ACS Publications, 1988.

Derek Walters. *The Art and Practice of Chinese Astrology*. New York: Simon and Schuster, 1987.

Juliet Sharman-Burke and Liz Greene. *The Mystic Tarot*. A deck of cards with an excellent instruction book by Derek Walters, Juliet Sharman-Burke, and Liz Greene.

Vickie Noble. *Motherpeace: A Way to the Goddess Through Myth, Art, and Tarot.* New York: Harper and Row, 1983.

Eileen Connolly. *A New Handbook for the Apprentice.* North Hollywood, Calif.: Newcastle, 1979.

Thomas Cleary, trans. *The Taoist I Ching.* Boston: Shambhala, 1986.

Carol K. Anthony. *The Philosophy of the I Ching.* Stow, Mass.: Anthony Publishing, 1981.

Ralph Blum. *The Book of Runes.* New York: Oracle Books, 1982.

Ralph Abraham and C. D. Shaw. *Dynamics: The Geometry of Behavior.* Santa Cruz: Ariel Press, 1982.

Michael Talbot. *Beyond the Quantum: A Journey to God and Reality in the New Scientific Revolution.* New York: Macmillan, 1987.

Stephen Hawking. *A Brief History of Time.* New York: Bantam, 1988.

Fritjof Capra. *The Tao of Physics.* New York: Bantam, 1984.

Joseph Campbell. *The Power of Myth.* New York: Doubleday, 1988.

Alan Watts. *In My Own Way.* New York: Vintage Books, 1973.

Alan Watts. *The Joyous Cosmology.* New York: Vintage Books, 1965.

Terence and Dennis McKenna. *The Invisible Landscape: Mind, Hallucinogens, and the I Ching.* New York: Seabury Press, 1975.

Joseph Chilton Pearce. *The Crack in the Cosmic Egg.* New York: Crown, 1976.

Yatri. *Unknown Man.* New York: Simon & Schuster, 1988.

Julian of Norwich. *Showings.* New York: Paulist Press, 1978.

James Joyce. *Finnegan's Wake.* New York: Penguin, 1976.

Chapter 13

Stephen LaBerge. *Lucid Dreams.* Los Angeles: Jeremy P. Tarcher, Inc., 1985.

Strephon Kaplan-Williams. *The Jungian-Senoi Dreamwork Manual.* Berkeley: Journey Press, 1980.

Bernie Siegal. *Love, Medicine, Miracles.* New York: Harper & Row, 1986.

Shakti Gawain. *Creative Visualization.* New York: Bantam Books, 1982.

Anees A. Sheikh, Ph.D., ed. *Anthology of Imagery Techniques.* Milwaukee: American Imagery Institute, 1986.

Robert A. Monroe. *Journeys Out of the Body.* New York: Anchor Press, 1977.

Robert A. Monroe. *Far Journeys*. New York: Dolphin Books, 1985.

Chapter 15

Michael Hutchinson. *The Book of Floating: Exploring the Private Sea*. San Francisco: Morrow, 1984.
John Lilly. *The Deep Self*. New York: Warner Books, 1977.